©Richard Kalina

*A view of the Globe stage, 1997*

## Contents

2    Shakespeare's Globe Exhibition
3    Sam's Story
9    The Globe Today
18   Shakespeare's London
25   Actors, Audiences, Architecture
33   Music
36   Symbolism
40   Rebuilding the Globe

48   The King's Men
52   Printing
60   Speaking Shakespeare
62   Dressing the Actors
72   Moving Ahead
74   Globe-to-Globe
76   Credits

*The Exhibition entrance on Bankside, opposite St Paul's Cathedral.*

*"an atmosphere that reflects the ethos of the Globe – informal, infectiously friendly, and compellingly inviting".*
TIME OUT

# Shakespeare's Globe Exhibition

For audiences and actors alike, performances or workshops at Shakespeare's Globe are an exciting and stimulating theatrical experience, quite unlike any other. The Exhibition, which occupies the Underglobe, the Cathedral-sized space under the theatre, is a pathway to that experience. From the moment you enter, you should at once be made aware of the significance of the Globe – both as a great circular space full of colour and drama, and the reflection of a global interest in Shakespeare and his theatre.

The journey that the modern visitor takes through the Exhibition tells a story that is as full of drama as any one of Shakespeare's plays. The story of how the new Globe came to be built and its important links with other countries, the exploration into how Shakespeare's own company operated on Bankside, the actors, the audiences, the music and clothing – these are all part of that story.

The Exhibition visit culminates in a guided tour or a virtual tour of the theatre. Our storytellers bring this extraordinary auditorium to life, using their expert knowledge and enthusiasm to introduce visitors to the space where many of Shakespeare's finest dramas were born.

The story they tell, however, has no ending. The Globe is a place of continuing experiment. The twin objectives of performance and education mean that the building is never empty; the Exhibition itself is always changing, the building-work continues and new discoveries are made by everyone who comes to the Globe, from America or Japan, Europe, Australia or right here in Southwark. It is this that should make a visit to Shakespeare's Globe Exhibition, and the centre as a whole, a unique experience and an inspiring one.

**David Marshall**
EXHIBITION DIRECTOR

*The inspiration for this extraordinary project first struck half a century ago.*

©Tom Boulting

*But it was a full twenty years before Sam was able to begin to work towards making his dream a reality.*

# Sam's Story

## Prologue

In 1949 the American actor-director Sam Wanamaker arrived in London, and made his way to Bankside to look for a monument to the Globe, the theatre where William Shakespeare had worked. On its site he found only a blackening bronze plaque on a brewery wall. Surely, he thought, Shakespeare's theatre deserved better than this...

©Brian Rybolt

*Sam Wanamaker beside the plaque marking the original Globe site. There is a replica of this plaque in the Exhibition.*

# Early Days

*The Museum at Bear Gardens*

**1969**

In 1969 Sam began in earnest his plans to rebuild the Globe close to its original site. It would, he hoped, be part of a large complex including education and research centres and an exhibition, as well as a cinema, flats, a pub, a car park, three hotels... The following year he founded the Globe Playhouse Trust.

With the help of the drama academic Diana Devlin he began to draw public attention to his project in the summer of 1972 with the first season of performances on the site. Among other attractions, this featured Keith Michell in a modern-dress *Hamlet*.

That same year Sam also opened the project's first exhibition, the Museum of the Shakespearean Stage at Bear Gardens (around the corner from the proposed theatre site), which his endlessly supportive wife Charlotte helped to set up and run.

**1972**

*Diana Devlin*

©Richard Olivier

*Charlotte Wanamaker*

©Tom Blau

**1973**

The second summer season, in 1973, was not the success it was expected to be. The highlight was to have been a production of *Antony and Cleopatra* starring Julian Glover and Vanessa Redgrave, but heavy rains flooded the tent and forced the whole season to be cancelled without completing its run. After less than three years, the Trust had become insolvent.

Diana Devlin, then secretary of the summer schools, had been warned:

*"Working for Sam, you will have to prepare large quantities of ready-mixed concrete to support his castles in the air. And be won't have money to pay for the concrete...."*

Never one to be deterred, Sam simply moved control of activities to an equivalent body, the World Centre for Shakespeare Studies.

**1974**

In 1974 Sam established the *Shakespeare Globe Centre USA* in Chicago. Today there are five other centres overseas, in Japan, Germany, Australia, New Zealand and Canada.

The second half of the 1970s was a difficult time for Sam and his dream. He was helped and supported by Theo Crosby, whom he had met in 1972; Theo was to become the project architect, as well as Sam's most faithful ally and – where necessary – his most honest critic.

Together they developed the idea of an inclusive international centre for Shakespeare, which they hoped could be financially self-sufficient. At its heart would be the reconstruction of Shakespeare's own theatre, built as far as possible just as the first Globe had been built four centuries earlier.

# The Struggle:
# Taking Decisions and Making Money

©Pentagram

*Theo Crosby*

Theo Crosby had come to England from his native South Africa in 1947. A founding partner of the design practice Pentagram, he worked with a mission: to bring life and humanity back to city architecture, with a balance between old and new. He met Sam early on in the project and from the outset was crucial to the development of the idea and the building of the theatre itself.

Sam believed strongly in the importance of engaging actively with scholars; so in 1981 he asked Professor Andrew Gurr of Reading University to set up an international academic committee to advise on the building project. Over the years the Globe rebuilding project benefited from the expertise and dedication of a large number of scholars who attended countless symposia – with architects and others – to debate the details of Sam's proposals. Most prominent among these academics were Professor Glynne Wickham and Professor John Orrell.

In 1981 at last it looked as though the dream might become a reality. An agreement was reached with Southwark Council to use a site on the bank of the Thames, a couple of hundred yards from the site of the original theatre. Somewhere had to be found to store the council's rubbish carts which had been kept there, but no-one envisaged any difficulties.

©Richard Kalina

*Andrew Gurr*

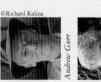

*John Orrell*

©John Price

*Glynne Wickham*

In 1982 the make-up of the council changed. Sam's project was accused of anti-social elitism by the new hard-line left-wing council, and by 1984 the agreement had been voided. "Shakespeare", said local councillor Tony Ritchie, "is tosh."

Sam brought a case against the council who had broken their agreement; in 1986 the case came to court and the decision was given in favour of the Globe. The site by the river was awarded to Sam's trust on a 125-year lease.

In 1984 Patrick Spottiswoode was appointed to reopen the museum – now the Shakespeare's Globe Museum – and to run the first education events.

©Richard Kalina

*Patrick Spottiswoode*

©Robert McBain

*Sam signals victory in the High Court case*

*Ann Ward*

1985 saw the founding of the Friends of Shakespeare's Globe, with Jane Lapotaire as its Honorary President and sympathetic Southwark councillor Ann Ward as one of its founding members. Sam often said that the project's eventual success would be only "due to the Friends' perseverance..."

In July 1983 a ceremony was held to dedicate the site. Of course, Sam did not yet have access to the site itself, but this didn't stop him; the ceremony was held regardless, just *outside* it! The Shakespeare Globe Trust was founded, under the chairmanship of Sir David Orr.

©Stewart Galloway

*Sir David Orr, Chairman of the Trustees*

# Building the Globe

*THE FRIENDS OF SHAKESPEARE'S GLOBE – Beginning with just a few members, this was originally intended to be primarily a fund-raising group, but quickly grew in membership and ambition. By the time the theatre opened in 1997 the Friends had over 7,000 members, had contributed a quarter of a million pounds towards the building and other projects, and had provided moral support, volunteers and enthusiasm in countless other ways.*

For years Sam had been thinking up dozens of fund-raising schemes, from international concert tours and specially commissioned poetry books to original private and corporate sponsorship opportunities. Prince Philip had agreed to be patron of the project, which through Sam's tireless campaigning managed to raise sufficient capital at least to *begin* work on the site.

---

**1987** brought the moment everybody had been waiting for through almost two decades, when the building work could at last begin. On 16th July Prince Philip was on the site to drive in the first oak foundation post.

The site was cleared at last, and on Shakespeare's birthday, April 23rd **1988** the official 'Globe Start' ceremony was held, with Judi Dench operating the earth-mover.

©Nicholas Garland

*Judi Dench and Sam in a cartoon drawing of the 'Globe Start' ceremony*

And by 1989 the new Globe's foundations were completed.

By a remarkable coincidence the same year brought two archaeological discoveries just down the road, both of enormous significance to the Globe project. In February the foundations of the Globe's neighbour-theatre The Rose were partially unearthed under what is now the Rose Court office building; and in October – a few dozen yards away – a fragment of the great Globe itself.

And that was not all. 1989 – a busy year by any standards! – also saw the official founding of the Globe Education department under Patrick Spottiswoode.

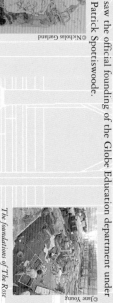
©Jane Young

*The foundations of The Rose*

The first milestone of the building itself was reached in 1992, with the building of the piazza above the foundations and the unveiling of the first two bays, in the presence of Prince Edward. The bays were the work of master carpenter Peter McCurdy, who took charge of all the project's timberwork.

©Bert Meredith

*HRH Prince Edward unveils the first two bays*

1987

1988

1989

1992

*When sorrows come, they come not single spies*
*But in battalions*
HAMLET, IV.5

©Markham & Froggett
*Mark Rylance*

©Richard Kalina
*The skeletal framework of the theatre in 1994*

Six years after the planting of the first foundation post, Prince Philip was back at the Globe, this time to unveil the magnificent New Zealand hangings which were to adorn the *frons scenae* (the back wall of the stage) for the opening festival. By now 13 of the 20 bays had been erected.

1994 also saw the filling out of the building's structure, with the construction of the walls (the largest lime plastering project in the U.K.) and thatching of the roof.

Theo Crosby died on September 12th. He too did not live to see the theatre finished, but he had at least been able to see most of the bays in place and the rest of the construction work well on its way to being completed.

A grant of £12.4 million awarded from the National Lottery in October 1995 made it possible to complete the building work under Theo Crosby's assistant and successor Jon Greenfield.

That summer the theatre had at last become ready to host its first audiences, and a temporary stage was ready for its first actors...

1995

1994

1993

©Doug Mackenzie
*The Bremer Shakespeare Company in* The Merry Wives of Windsor

By the time the Bremer Shakespeare Company came over to perform their *Merry Wives of Windsor* on the site in 1993, four of the theatre's bays had been erected and it seemed that Sam Wanamaker's dream would at long last become a reality.

Sam died on December 18th, 1993. Although he did not live to see his project completed, he did know that his twenty-five year struggle had been worthwhile. He knew that before long Shakespeare's Globe theatre would again be 'the glorie of the Banke'.

## Open for Business

The Artistic Directorate, a committee of international actors, directors and other theatre practitioners was formed. In June 1995 they appointed actor-director Mark Rylance (who had performed on the site in 1991) Artistic Director of the Globe as of the following summer. Summer 1995 also saw a Workshop Season in the substantially completed theatre on a temporary stage. This experiment, which included visits by 30 outside groups, aroused fierce debates among academics and theatre practitioners.

©Bill Mackenzie

*Sir Michael Perry was appointed by Sam Wanamaker Chairman of the International Shakespeare Globe Centre. As a senior executive of Unilever he was able to provide the financial skills so much needed at the time.*

*He later became Chairman of the Trust.*

# Sam's Story

Triumphes and Mirth, *Festival of Firsts*

©Richard Kalina

©Nik Milner

The following summer the 'Prologue' Season saw Mark Rylance back on the Globe stage in *The Two Gentlemen of Verona*, directed by Jack Shepherd and featuring Lenny James and Anastasia Hille. This working season again led to further debate, and to changes to the design of the stage – in particular to the size and position of the two pillars supporting the 'heavens' (the roof structure above the stage), and in consequence the whole structure of 'the heavens' themselves.

Another traditional craft was brought onto the site in 1997, when Richard Quinnell, sponsored by the Ford Motor Company, brought together an international team of metalworkers to forge the splendid Bankside Gates that feature the flora and fauna of Shakespeare's plays.

By the spring of 1997 the theatre was ready for its grand opening. Well, *almost* ready. All that was missing was the redesigned stage, with the *frons scenae* and the heavens, which were all completed, painted and thatched in April and May.

©Malcolm Bennett

The Groundling Gates sponsored by the Ford Foundation. Detailed images from the gates; the mermaid and the mole.

©Steve Waters

This costume displayed in the exhibition was made for Jane Lapotaire (as Elizabeth I) to greet Elizabeth II

A banner flying to celebrate the Festival of Firsts

©Richard Kalina

Zoë Wanamaker

At last on June 8th the Opening Season was launched. As part of the two-week-long 'Festival of Firsts', Her Majesty the Queen and H.R.H. Prince Philip attended a specially commissioned masque, *Triumphes and Mirth*, on June 12th to celebrate the opening of Shakespeare's Globe Theatre. Neither Sam Wanamaker nor Theo Crosby was there, nor was Sam's wife Charlotte who had died earlier in the year; but they were all in the audience's minds as Zoë Wanamaker – Sam and Charlotte's daughter – stepped onto the new stage to speak the lines from the Prologue to *Henry V*:

*O! for a Muse of fire, that would ascend*
*The brightest heaven of invention;*
*A kingdom for a stage, princes to act*
*And monarchs to behold the swelling scene.*

*... But pardon, gentles all,*
*The flat, unraised spirits that hath dared*
*On this unworthy scaffold to bring forth*
*So great an object: can this cockpit hold*
*The vasty fields of France? or may we cram*
*Within this wooden O the very casques*
*That did affright the air at Agincourt?*
*O, pardon! Since a crooked figure may*
*Attest in little place a million;*
*And let us, ciphers to this great accompt,*
*On your imaginary forces work...*

# The Globe Today

*Much of the criticism that was levelled at Sam Wanamaker and the Globe project in its early days hinged on the mistaken idea that it was to be either a museum-piece or a Disney-like fantasy 'experience'. The press attacked the concept, scholars questioned the validity of the whole project. It was difficult to explain what the objectives were until there was something concrete to back up the philosophy.*

©Richard Kalina

Now that the Globe is in operation, as a centre of education and performance, there is no barrier to demonstrating the real excitement of continual experiment with the works of Shakespeare and his contemporaries. Now audiences, students and visitors to the exhibition can see for themselves how the working atmosphere of the building on London's Bankside brings us a clearer understanding of the golden age of English literature.

All year round Shakespeare's Globe Exhibition offers a lively illustrated pathway into the world of the Globe, telling the story of Shakespeare's workplace through a variety of media and interactive displays. Visits to the Exhibition are complemented with tours of the theatre itself, led by knowledgeable and enthusiastic guides.

The twin objectives of education and theatre practice run throughout both the summer and winter seasons.

# Summer: the Theatre Season

*The summer season runs for six months, from April to September. During that time, visitors to the exhibition and theatre tours often find themselves looking in on rehearsals, or on the verse, voice and movement training which all the actors undergo; there are performances in the theatre most afternoons and evenings, six days a week.*

© John Tramper

*Merchant of Venice, 1998*

A major part of the excitement of the Globe is the 'large intimacy' of the theatre, where the audience of over 1500 surrounds the stage and is never far from the action. The fact that there is no roof over the yard and plays are performed in daylight also brings actors and audience together in a shared experience, rain or shine. Whereas in a darkened auditorium each member of the audience relates to the performance as an individual, in the Globe the visual excitement of the space and the audience within it becomes a vital part of the occasion. Communication between actor and audience and the story telling of the play and the characters are more immediate than in a conventional theatre.

© Donald Cooper

*As You Like It, 1998*

Actors need to be able to let their thoughts be expressed by their bodies. As Master of Movement, I help them to become aware that this expression requires both physical freedom and alert stillness. Like the strings of a musical instrument, if their bodies are tense, their actions may seem sharp, if they are too relaxed, flat. 'Fine tuning' brings the right muscle tone, ease and grace, so they can discover the 'true note' of the characters they are playing. Through movement work, alone and with each other, an actor can strive to make communication clearer, and to embody Hamlet's words: "What a piece of work is a man, in form and moving how express and admirable, in action how like an angel…"

GLYNN MACDONALD, MASTER OF MOVEMENT

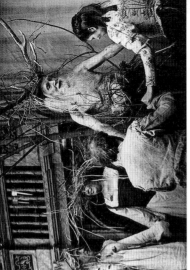

©Sheila Burnett

*As You Like It, 1998*

Shakespeare's company was set up and managed by actors. Actors still form a large part of the work at the Globe today; as well as having two or three companies to perform in the repertory system, actors lead workshops, Bankside 'walkshops' and the guided theatre tours; they work with student groups in summer school and with the younger children who join in 'ChildsPlay' activities that parallel the performance in the theatre.

*The Globe is an actor-athlete's space.*

MARCELLO MAGNI

*As Master of Voice my job is to examine and inspire creative audibility within the stage life of the Globe actor. The demands of the Globe are vocally challenging, so a robust, relaxed vocal physique must be acquired; this allows actors to produce the necessary clarity to play the full emotional life of their characters within a range that can be easily heard by those present, and equips them with a technique to support them through a five-month season of playing. As in Shakespeare's day, an audience arrives to "hear a play", so an actor is excited and enthused into exploring a dynamic, naturalistic form of 'magnetic' story-telling – it is this form that draws the audience into the spirit of the play.*

STEWART PEARCE, MASTER OF VOICE

©John Tramper

*Merchant of Venice, 1998*

*The Globe is a very helpful space to the actor, because of the real people who are there, because they are so empowered. As the architecture is so unusual, it will take some time, I think, for the audience to explore fully how they should behave here. They do sometimes become annoyed by the distractions here compared to other theatres, but also they are open to discover that they may be able to behave differently here too. As the actors become more confident, they realise it is OK to pause for a moment and wait for the drama that is happening amongst the audience to play itself out, before picking up and carrying on with the drama on the stage...*

MARK RYLANCE

©John Tramper

*Julius Caesar*, 1999

There is often a common theme running through the choice of plays and that theme is picked up and explored in a series of play-readings, lectures and talks with the actors, designers or directors. The particular architecture of the Globe also encourages new plays. The 1999 season saw the first specially commissioned play at the Globe, Peter Oswald's verse-drama *Augustine's Oak*.

*The idea of being able to see everybody in the audience was completely unknown territory – it was terrifying! However, when I first stepped out in front of an audience, I thought almost immediately, 'This isn't frightening at all.'*

JULES MELVIN

©Donald Cooper

*King Lear*, 2001

©Sheila Burnett

*Kathakali King Lear*, 1999

©Sheila Burnett

*Umabatha: The Zulu Macbeth, 2001*

©Donald Cooper

*Macbeth, 2001*

*The groundlings have their own extraordinary agenda, their own playfulness and a tremendous desire to be included. There's a great seduction that comes from them, to which I freely admit I have succumbed, partly to explore it and partly just to enjoy it. It's really raw, and it's quite scary, like a bearpit; there's something quite gladiatorial about the Globe as a playing-space.*

JASPER BRITTON

Experimental productions and performance styles from other countries also feature as part of the summer season.

Although the summer is the time when the theatre comes into its own, with audiences and performers filling the space, educational activities continue throughout the season.

©John Tramper

©Sheila Burnett

*The Tempest, 2000*

# Winter: the Education Season

The Globe has at its core one of the most extensive education programmes of any U.K. arts organisation. It offers unparalleled access to the experiences of a community of theatre practitioners who are engaged in learning what it is to create a play on this unique stage. Every year over 50,000 people across all age groups benefit from Globe Education's extraordinary year-round range of workshops, courses, lectures, staged readings and distance learning programmes.

Globe Education strives to uncover the 'soul of lively action' within every aspect of its work. This is achieved in large part through collaboration with actors and other key theatre professionals. Their practical experience of preparing Shakespeare for performance encourages participants to approach his stories and language actively.

The Globe Education flag flies above the Theatre from October to March and, during the Education Season, all workshops include exploratory work on the Globe stage. The emphasis is always on how to lift Shakespeare's language off the page and into life. It is also a continuous process of helping people to discover the playhouse in the plays.

The *Lively Action* programme provides half-day workshops and study days for primary and secondary school students throughout the year. The emphasis is on exploring Shakespeare's plays actively within the context of his playhouse and the world beyond the playhouse door. Teachers can benefit from the range of in-service training opportunities at the Globe, from conferences and MA modules to summer institutes. Globe Education's web page (at www.shakespeares-globe.org) also provides an invaluable resource for teachers across the world.

©Sheila Burnett

*Children in the theatre yard*

©Sheila Burnett

*Active learning on stage*

Globe Education has forged links with a number of special schools and offers *Touch Tours* of the theatre for both the visually impaired and students with severe learning difficulties. It runs After School Clubs and a summer 'university' for local children. The annual *Our Theatre* project involves Southwark primary and secondary school students, assisted over several months by Globe Education practitioners (most of whom are professional actors), in the development of scenes from Shakespeare, which are presented to large and enthusiastic audiences in the Globe Theatre itself.

Schools across the world can share in the Globe's programmes via *GlobeLink*, Globe Education's membership association. Members can participate in video-conferences and a variety of distance learning activities via the web. Over one hundred schools and universities participate annually in GlobeLink's *Adopt an Actor* scheme, which offers students around the world the chance to adopt one of ten actors in the Globe Theatre Company.

©Sheila Burnett

*Globe Education actors leading a workshop*

©Sheila Burnett

*A visiting production at a Globe Education INSET day*

©Sheila Burnett

*'Read not dead' – staged readings in the old Bear Gardens theatre*

Students follow their actors from the first day of rehearsal to the last performance, asking and answering questions and sharing in the discoveries made during the process of creating a production.

For those wanting insights into the intricate worlds of clothing, design and music at the Globe, there are seminar demonstrations led by practitioners actually involved in creating the productions at the Globe. Undergraduates can benefit from introductory lectures and workshops exploring the subtle interplay that exists between actors, audiences and architecture – the three 'A's' – which give productions in this theatre such resonance. Undergraduate semester courses exploring 'Text and Performance' and 'Theatre Design' are also provided throughout the year. Globe Education has also devised a special MA in 'Shakespearean Studies: Text and Playhouse' in conjunction with King's College, London.

©Sheila Burnett

©Sheila Burnett

*Young musicians in the Globe*

©Sheila Burnett

*A Globe Education workshop*

*A Southwark 'Walkshop' on Bankside*

Modules are provided for a variety of MFA programmes for universities in the U.K. and abroad drawing on the expertise of the Globe's Masters of Movement, Voice and Verse.

Members of the general public can benefit throughout the year from an array of lectures, courses and special events. During the Theatre Season, *Globe Walkshops*, introductory lectures and *Talking Theatre* sessions with members of the Globe Theatre Company are presented every week. On Saturdays, 8-11 year olds can join *ChildsPlay* workshops before being taken into the theatre to see the last twenty minutes of the play that their parents are watching.

Lectures, seminars, evening classes and occasional film screenings are organised during the Education Season around chosen themes. Staged readings of lesser-known plays by Shakespeare's contemporaries complement the themes. It is Globe Education's aim to record all the non-Shakespeare plays of the period with professional casts over the next 25 years. Some of these plays are edited alongside the staged readings by young scholars and are published as 'Globe Quartos' by Nick Hern Books.

*Sam Wanamaker founded Globe Education in 1989 so that a range of education programmes could be in place in advance of the opening of the Globe Theatre. He insisted that Globe Education should serve local, national and international communities and provide workshops and courses for people of all ages and abilities. Globe Education seeks to fulfil his aim that the Globe Theatre should be open to all.*

# Shakespeare's London

### St Paul's Cathedral

The Cathedral that Shakespeare would have known was the fourth on this site, the first three all having been destroyed by fire. This fourth was a massive Gothic building, and boasted the highest spire ever built at the time. But from the Reformation it began to fall into disrepair. The spire was struck by lightning in 1561 and never rebuilt, the High Altar was demolished and the Nave became a bustling thoroughfare and meeting-place for tradesmen. Elizabeth I attended services here, and donated money towards the building's upkeep, but never enough to restore it to its former glory.

The Cathedral we see opposite the Globe today was built by Christopher Wren at the end of the 17th century, after the fourth was destroyed in the Fire of London.

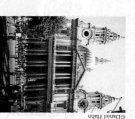
©Daniel Hahn

### Borough Market

With a thousand years' activity behind it, Borough Market is the oldest market in London. In Shakespeare's day the market also sold grain, fish and cattle. Merchants from all over Europe would travel into the capital from the coastal ports and trade here; they would stay the night in one of the many inns in Southwark, the best known of which – The Tabard – features in Chaucer's *Canterbury Tales*.

©Daniel Hahn

### Southwark Cathedral

There has probably been a church on this site for over a thousand years. In the Middle Ages it formed part of the Priory of St Mary Overies (meaning 'over the river'); following the dissolution of the monasteries by Henry VIII it became the parish church of St Saviour. The parishioners of Southwark finally bought it from James I in 1614. Playwrights John Fletcher and Philip Massinger are buried here, as is Shakespeare's brother Edmund. In 1912 a memorial to Shakespeare was erected in the Cathedral, and a plaque to the memory of Sam Wanamaker was unveiled alongside it in 1994.

©Daniel Hahn

*Citizens of London; from the 'Civitates Orbis Terrarum' of Braun and Hogenberg, 1572*

Elizabethan London was a thriving, rapidly expanding city. It doubled in size in the second half of the 16th century, and by 1650 had doubled again to a population of 400,000, making it the largest city in the world. By this time it had expanded well beyond the limits of the part of old London we call The City today.

The city streets, densely packed, thronged with carriers' carts, coaches and pedestrians. There were large markets at Cheapside and Eastcheap, where Londoners could buy local produce and imported goods brought up the river by foreign merchants.

London's tradesmen were organised into guilds, or 'livery companies', of which there were about fifty in Shakespeare's day (there are twice that number today). Each of these was responsible for maintaining standards and setting prices. Many of the trades were associated with particular areas. There are reminders of this in the street names that survive today – Bread Street, Milk Street, Ironmonger Lane, Poultry, Hosier Lane...

Officially, the capital of England was not the City of London but the City of Westminster. The government of the City of London was in the hands of the Lord Mayor and the Aldermen and 'Councilmen'. They were elected from among London business people, as is still the custom today. The city was divided into Wards and their representatives formed the Court of Common Council, the effective governing body. These divisions are still in place today.

Convent garden    S. Clement

Somerset E    Arundel house    Peter house    Temple stayrs    Temple    Blackfreyars    Baynards Castle    Paulus wharfe

The Globe

Beere bayting

S. y.<sup>e</sup> Waterhouse

S. Pauwls Church

S. Andre in Holborne

Newgat

Boo Church

Guildhall

4. Alhallouws y.<sup>e</sup> great

Queene hythe

The 3. Cranes

Stiliard

Cole harbour

the Eel Ships

LON

T H A M E S I S

winchester house

Sout

### The Tower of London

Begun in the reign of William the Conqueror, the Tower has been a famous symbol of royal power for over nine centuries. Many monarchs chose to live part of their time there, and all used it for housing the out of favour, sometimes indefinitely. In Shakespeare's day the Tower housed a number of distinguished prisoners, including Walter Ralegh and Guy Fawkes. Besides the prison and the notorious execution block, the Tower has also housed the Royal Wardrobe, the Mint, the Armoury and the Royal Menagerie.

*Passengers crossing the Thames in a wherry, by Michael van Meer*

*A frost fair on the Thames. A model on loan from the Museum of London*

### London Bridge

Until 1750 London Bridge was the only river crossing in the London area. So for those unable to pay the boat fare, it was the only means of access to the theatres, taverns, brothels and bear-baiting rings south of the Thames. The bridge itself was celebrated as a great gem in the city's crown; but it was also over-crowded with shops, houses and people, and must have been dirty, noisy and unpleasant. And certainly the rotting heads of traitors mounted on stakes at the southern end cannot have helped...

# The Thames

## *The Pool of London*

In Elizabethan England the lower Thames was crowded with ships sailing to and from the rest of Europe and Scandinavia. This trade link, which was vital to the city, had its heart at the Pool of London, the wider part of the river just to the east of London Bridge. The Pool of London was effectively the capital's main port from Roman times until the nineteenth century.

## *Crossing the river*

For those who wanted to avoid the bustle of London Bridge – and could afford the fare – it was possible to cross the river by boat. These boats, called 'wherries' crossed from one set of landing steps to another, and ferrymen would attract trade crying 'Westward ho!' or 'Eastward ho!', depending on whether they were travelling up or downstream.

## *Frost fairs*

During long periods of cold weather the Thames would ice over above London Bridge and impromptu 'frost fairs' were set up on the frozen river. In 1564-5, Elizabeth I visited a fair on the frozen Thames, where entertainment included dancing and archery.

So powerful were these 'City Fathers' in Shakespeare's day that the acting companies found it better to operate outside their jurisdiction, in what were known as 'The Liberties', areas immediately outside the city and originally under church privilege. Although they were beyond the jurisdiction of the city authorities, the players on Bankside were still subject to the rule of the Master of Revels, who was responsible for censoring and licensing all plays for public performance.

If the city authorities were bothered about performances or the behaviour of crowds outside the playhouses, they had to send letters to the magistrates of Middlesex (to the north) or Surrey (to the south) to ask them to intervene.

This was particularly important in times of plague when all public gatherings except for worship were forbidden. When there were more than thirty deaths a week the theatres were closed.

*London, by Claes Jan Visscher, 1616*

Guildhall Library

*...To the present stay and final suppressing of the said stage plays as well at the Theatre, Curtain and Bankside as in all other places in and about the city. In time of sickness it is found by experience that many, having sores but not yet heart-sick, take occasion to walk abroad and re-create themselves by hearing a play, whereby others are infected...*
FROM THE LORD MAYOR AND ALDERMEN TO THE QUEEN'S PRIVY COUNCIL, 28TH JULY 1597

There were very few years when closures did not occur and the London acting companies then had to take to the road, where they were not always welcome, coming as they did from a plague city.

J. Alhallows barking

The Tower.

Eastwambogle

Tower Wharfe

S. Olafe

*Wenceslaus Hollar's 'Long View' of London.*

*Completed in the 1640s, this panorama shows the second Globe before it was pulled down.*

*Of the two arenas shown The Globe is the one on the left – the names of The Globe and the 'beere-bayting' have been accidently reversed by the engraver.*

# Bankside: The Theatres

*This detail from John Norden's panorama of London shows Bankside around 1600. Among the open fields, gardens and lanes stand four large, circular buildings. To the extreme left is the Swan playhouse; in the centre the Bear Garden with the Rose beside it (named as the Stare or Star) and at the lower edge the newly built Globe with its thatched roof. Winchester House is clearly shown (with the number 20 above it) near the church of St Mary Overye, now Southwark Cathedral, at the foot of London Bridge.*

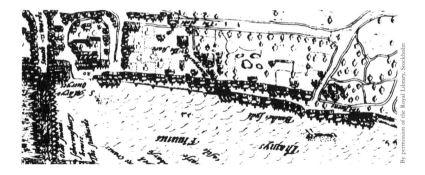

By this time Bankside had become the heart of the capital's theatre world. It was a perfect place to set up a playhouse. All those whose activities the city authorities had tried to suppress had made their way here; so the area also housed a large number of taverns, brothels, bear-baiting arenas, and other recreations frowned upon by the more puritan citizens on the north bank of the river. One of the most famous of the 'houses of easy virtue' was 'Hollands Leaguer' which lay near the Swan playhouse and catered for a very wealthy and exclusive clientele.

Much of the land belonged to the Bishop of Winchester, so it was his responsibility to control the brothels, whose inmates were known as 'Winchester Geese'. He also maintained a prison on his land, known as The Clink. This remains a generic nickname for prisons today.

*A panorama of Bankside today*

*On September 21st after lunch, about two o'clock, I and my party crossed the water, and there in the house with the thatched roof witnessed an excellent performance of the tragedy of the first emperor Julius Caesar ...*
THOMAS PLATTER, 1599

# The Museum of London and the Globe

*In 1989 a team from the Museum of London Archaeological Survey were able to carry out partial excavations of the two theatre foundations discovered on the Bankside: the Globe and the Rose. MoLAS's work over the years has been invaluable in teaching us about the playhouses themselves and life in Shakespeare's London in general. Much of Bankside has already been excavated, and literally hundreds of relics of life in Shakespeare's day have been found, from clay pipes and crockery to animal skulls and more…*

A number of these discoveries are now on display in the Globe Exhibition.

*Leatherwork was one of the many industries important on Bankside*

# A Feast at Bermondsey

*In Shakespeare's day the countryside came very near the city walls. Just across the Thames from the Tower of London lay fields that had once been part of the great abbey at Bermondsey. This painting by a Flemish exile, Joris Hoefnagel, from the 1570s, shows the many different strata of English society; however, it also raises a great many questions.*

Is there a wedding going on? A feast is being prepared. Are those giant pies that the serving men and women are carrying?

There is certainly music and dancing. There are viols of different sizes. Is the man on the extreme right playing a pipe, or smoking one?

In spite of the surrounding gaiety a man sits in the stocks.

There are some very outlandish costumes. People from many nations congregated near the port of London, which lies where the ship may be seen in the background.

Children were dressed as adults. Babies were often swaddled tightly until they could sit and crawl. Young boys wore skirts until they were 'breeched' at about seven years old.

Taverns were distinguished by having a bush mounted on a pole outside. The one here is very tall, perhaps so that it can be seen from the river.

# Actors, Audiences, Architecture

## Travelling players

*In Shakespeare's day, companies of actors would travel throughout England and Northern Europe attracting large audiences at fairs and festivals.*

*Detail showing an open-air stage in Northern Europe, from a print by R. Booms, 1618.*

Temporary stages on high trestles catered for a standing audience.

Clowns with bladders on sticks kept order.

Curtained entrances backed the stage.

Costumes were a major part of the company's wealth. Classical, Royal and Fantasy characters all had distinctive dress.

Actors and musicians went through the streets in procession to drum up an audience.

Travelling companies required a licence to perform in any town and to prevent their arrest as 'vagabonds'.

Queen Elizabeth issued the first known licence in 1574 to the Earl of Leicester's Men, one of whom was the businessman James Burbage.

In 1576 Burbage built the first purpose-built playhouse, adjoining a barn in the fields to the north of the City of London. Taking the name from the Roman amphitheatres, he called it 'The Theatre'.

# The Playhouses

> *The Theatre had roofed galleries surrounding a yard, entrance doors and stair-towers for access to the upper galleries, all of which made the collection of money easier than in a public space. In many respects it resembled one of the arenas for animal-baiting with dogs which provided popular entertainment at the time.*

*Bear Baiting in a Fechthaus (fights arena) built in Nurnberg in 1628. The arena was also used for other displays, including performances by English travelling players.*

Very soon other playhouses followed. In 1577 The Curtain, owned by Henry Lanham, opened nearby and served Burbage's company as a second playing space when the lease on The Theatre's land expired.

Ten years later Philip Henslowe built The Rose on the south bank of the Thames, an area already known for a variety of entertainments, and which stood outside the jurisdiction of the City authorities. The Rose was followed by several other playhouses, notably The Swan in 1595 and the first Globe which opened in 1599.

The first Globe was built by Burbage's company using timbers, taken secretly over the Christmas season, from The Theatre, which had been banned from use by the landlord.

Burbage's company, now installed on Bankside, included an actor/playwright called William Shakespeare. It is his Globe that we have tried to reconstruct today.

*A much enlarged detail showing the site of The Theatre; from Abram Booth's 'View of the Cittye of London from the North towards the Sowth'.*

Before the appearance of the first purpose-built playhouses, acting companies would often perform in the courtyards of inns, which provided the basis for purpose-built innyard playhouses (like the Red Lion, which is considered the first public playhouse). These places were particularly convenient for touring companies. It was easier to control audiences here than in the open market squares, and easier to ensure that everyone attending the play had paid. Innyards also provided galleries and windows for select audiences. A similar galleried inn still to be found near the Globe is the old George Inn just south of London Bridge.

Public playhouses like The Rose and The Globe were large and could hold up to three thousand people. The stage was five feet high and roofed over to protect actors and their costumes. The roof was supported on pillars, entrances were from the tiring house (tiring = attiring or dressing), there was a balcony above and space below the stage, and the whole decoration of the theatre was magnificently colourful.

The popularity and magnificence of these theatres attracted some rather harsh criticism.

Daylight performances meant actors could make direct contact with the audience. There was no director as such, so actors were very much in charge of their own characterisations. The companies owned a large repertoire of plays and in Shakespeare's time they gave a different play every afternoon.

*the cause of plagues is sinne, if you looke to it well: and the cause of sinne are playes: therefore the cause of plagues are playes...*
THOMAS WHITE, SERMON, 1577

Guildhall Library

*The misnamed second Globe with a tiled roof; from Wenceslaus Hollar's 'Long View'*

In 1613 The Globe burned down during a performance of Shakespeare's *Henry VIII* when a stage cannon in the turret above the heavens was fired. The wadding that held the gunpowder in place fell flaming out and set the thatch on fire.

*.... Wherein yet nothing did perish but wood and straw, and a few forsaken cloaks; only one man had his breeches set on fire, that would perhaps have broiled him, if he had not, by the benefit of a provident wit, put it out with bottle ale.*
SIR HENRY WOTTON

One year later a second Globe, this time with a tiled roof, was completed on the foundations of the first.

*Actor-clown Will Kemp dancing from London to Norwich*

# Performance

*...a strutting player, whose conceit*
*Lies in his hamstring, and doth think it rich*
*To hear the wooden dialogue and sound*
*'Twixt his stretch'd footing and the scaffoldage.*

TROILUS AND CRESSIDA, I.3

Whether in prose or verse, plays contained much action. Actors were expert swordsmen and dancers and often could sing and play an instrument as well. Bloodthirsty effects such as heads on poles, wounds, ghosts and devils were all graphically produced; flying, trapdoors and magic tricks were used to make objects or people appear and disappear.

*No longer needed for warfare in the sixteenth century, swordplay developed into a courtly accomplishment. Italian, French and Spanish styles of weaponry and elaborate rules of conduct were established. Many outdoor playhouses were used as venues for feats of arms, and plays such as* Hamlet *often required actors to demonstrate a high level of skill in swordsmanship.*

Traditionally acting companies were all men. Boys played pages and girls' parts, while young men with light voices took the leading women's roles. Older men may have played old women as well as the comic parts.

Acting companies included the boys, hired men for small parts, musicians, a wardrobe keeper (tire-man), stage keeper and book holder. The book holder kept the play scripts and set out the order of scenes, lists of entrances, stage-properties and sound effects.

Interactive displays in the exhibition gallery show a wide range of staging effects and stage practices.

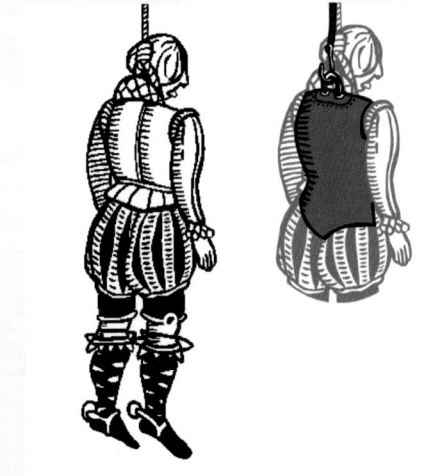

*An effective stage hanging, and the leather harness that made the effect possible. Two images from the Exhibition's interactive displays.*

# The Audiences

*O! it offends me to the soul to hear a robustious periwig-pated fellow tear a passion to tatters, to very rags, to split the ears of the groundlings, who for the most part are capable of nothing but inexplicable dumb-shows and noise...*
HAMLET, III.2

Groundlings were the standing members of the audience in the public playhouses. For one penny (the price of a loaf of bread) you could stand in the open yard, but if privacy and a roof overhead were important to you, then a seat in the galleries or even in the 'gentlemen's rooms' on either side near the stage could be obtained for further payment.

*Whoever cares to stand below pays only one English penny but if he wishes to sit he enters by another door and pays another penny...*
THOMAS PLATTER, 1599

Food and drink were on sale and performances were given in the afternoon.

*The best treat was to see and stare at so much nobility in such excellent array that they seemed so many princes, listening as silently and soberly as possible, and many honourable and handsome ladies come there very freely and take their seats among the men without hesitation.*
ORAZIO BUSINO, CHAPLAIN OF THE VENETIAN EMBASSY, DURING A VISIT TO THE FORTUNE PLAYHOUSE IN 1617

Visitors from overseas were often surprised by the behaviour of audiences, intent on following the play, even in the rough-and-tumble of the yard.

Audiences would applaud at any notable event during the play, but it was only at the end that they could be really disruptive. There was often a 'jig' – a comic song-and-dance story – and the company would announce the next play in the repertoire. The audience would show their likes and dislikes of the choice by calling out, whistling and even throwing things, as happened when the Venetian Ambassador visited The Curtain in 1613.

# Playing Spaces

*The adaptability of the acting companies and the variety of locations for performances are clearly illustrated in the three models commissioned for the Exhibition and created by Paul Wells.*

© Paul Wells

*The model of the Boar's Head in progress*

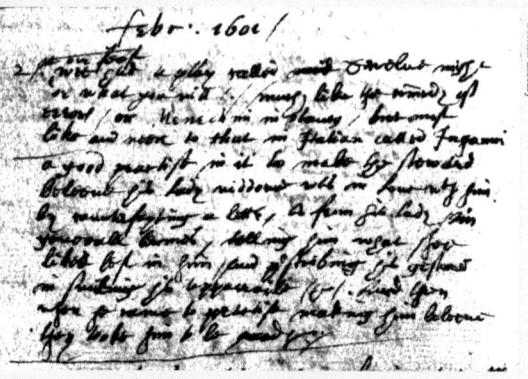

British Library

*John Manningham describes in his diary the first recorded performance of* Twelfth Night, *in Middle Temple Hall, on February 2nd, 1602.*

© Tom Boulting

*The Boar's Head, Whitechapel*

© Tom Boulting

*The Rose*

© Tom Boulting

*Middle Temple Hall*

- **The Boar's Head, Whitechapel**
  Converted into an open stage with galleries in 1598. The early use of innyards, as an alternative to street theatre, allowed actors and publicans to charge entry prices.

- **The Rose**
  This model is an informed guess as to what this early purpose-built playhouse looked like, based on the archaeological discovery of the foundations in 1989. The site in Park Street, around the corner from Shakespeare's Globe, is open to visitors.

- **Middle Temple Hall**
  This magnificent hall just north of the Thames was the setting for a performance of Shakespeare's *Twelfth Night* on the 2nd of February, 1602. The Middle Temple Hall still stands, much as it was in Shakespeare's day.

# Indoor performances

*From earliest times halls such as the one at Middle Temple were used for the performance of 'Interludes', often by professional players, between the courses of feasts.*

*Duke Theseus*   *Say, what abridgement have you for this evening?*
*What masque? What music? How shall we beguile*
*The lazy time if not with some delight?*

A MIDSUMMER NIGHT'S DREAM, V.1

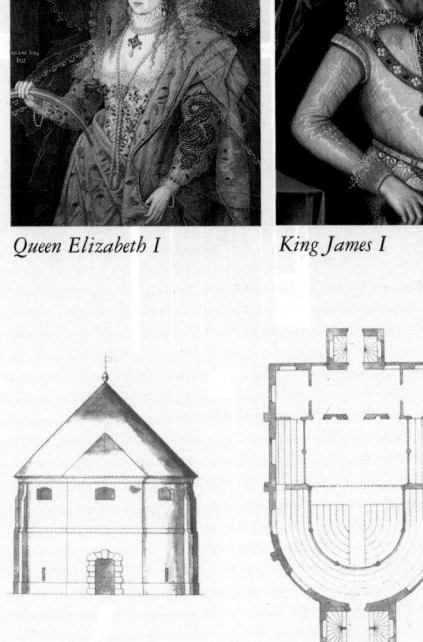

The Marquess of Salisbury, Hatfield House   ©National Maritime Museum

*Queen Elizabeth I*          *King James I*

For winter quarters and to satisfy the needs of the Court and the patrons whose servants they were, actors looked for indoor playing spaces. Queen Elizabeth I and King James I both commanded performances for special occasions such as the visit of a foreign ambassador. The Christmas season at Court always included the performance of the current London hits by the leading companies.

In 1596 James Burbage built a new playhouse in a hall in the Blackfriars, near St Paul's. He meant it to be the replacement for his Theatre whose lease was to expire the following year. But he was blocked from using the Blackfriars by the local residents, so the company built The Globe instead. The Blackfriars was used once a week by a boys' company from 1600 to 1608 when the Globe company retrieved it. Subsequently they played at the Globe in the summer and the Blackfriars in the winter.

British Library

Inigo Jones's designs for an indoor theatre were incorporated into the Globe Centre. These designs show a small, classic playhouse comparable to many continental theatres.

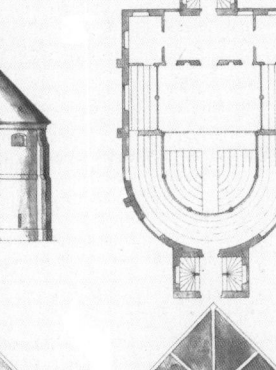

By permission of the Provost & Fellows of Worcester College, Oxford

*Designs by Inigo Jones for an indoor theatre, possibly the Cockpit, Drury Lane*

*Entry of the players into a manor house; from Moyses Walens,* Album Amicorum

## Court Masques

*And while the public playhouses were seeing the dramatic works of Shakespeare and his fellows brought to the stage for the first time, the Court of James I saw the development of a whole new kind of entertainment: the Court Masque.*

*Inigo Jones, self-portrait*

Members of the Court themselves would appear in these private evening performances, often dressed in the most fantastical costumes. Unlike the professional acting companies which were all male, women often had leading roles. Major speaking parts were given to the leading professional players.

The costumes, scenery and stages for many of the masques at the Stuart Court were designed by Inigo Jones, the King's Surveyor. Jones drew inspiration from Italian Renaissance theatre to create stunning sets that presented a series of perspective cut-outs, often within a proscenium arch, quite unlike the scenic conventions at the Globe. His designs would complement the words of playwrights such as Ben Jonson, and the music, dance and lighting, to magical effect.

*Setting and costume design b[y] Inigo Jones for* The Masque o[f] Oberon

## MUSIC in the Court Masque

*Noble patrons sponsored composers and poets as well as painters and actors. Music for the court masques – which were the fore-runners of opera and ballet – was provided by composers such as the Italian emigré Ferrabosco, who worked with Inigo Jones and Ben Jonson.*

Harmony between monarchs, and between monarchs and the nation, is the most important motif in any court masque. This passage is taken from Sir William D'Avenant's masque *Salmacida Spolia* (designed by Jones), in 1640, the last masque before the civil war.

*So musical, as to all ears
Doth seem the music of the spheres,
As you unto each other still
Tuning your thoughts to either's will.*

*All that are harsh, all that are rude,
Are by your harmony subdu'd
Yet so into obedience wrought
As if not forc'd to it but taught.*

# Music in the Public Playhouses

| *Shakespeare's plays are rich with references to music.*

At the Globe instrumental music could be used to fulfil a myriad of functions, from percussive music to evoke a battle scene, to instrumental music to create a party atmosphere as at the ball where Romeo and Juliet first meet.

Music may have been exotic or sinister, as when hautboys are played under the stage in *Antony and Cleopatra* to signify the departure of the god Hercules from Antony. Or it may have been magical, as at the end of *The Winter's Tale*; when Paulina calls for music it seems as though it is the music itself that brings the statue of Hermione to life.

> *Music, awake her: strike!*
> *'Tis time; descend; be stone no more; approach.*
> *Strike all that look upon with marvel.*
> THE WINTER'S TALE, V.3

*John McEnery playing and singing, in the role of the Fool in* King Lear

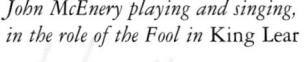

## Songs

*There are about a hundred songs and extracts from songs in Shakespeare's plays. Many could have been accompanied on the lute or viol, perhaps by the singer himself, as Balthasar does in* Much Ado About Nothing.

*Richard Tarlton, the actor, playing a pipe and tabor*

## Musicians

*It is possible that actors (like many ladies and gentlemen) would have been trained to play musical instruments. This meant that some on-stage music may have been provided by the actors themselves. Ensemble music was usually provided by hired professionals, or 'waits'.*

*A procession of musicians*

The acting companies had their own collections of instruments. A list of properties for the Admiral's Men includes a dozen instruments of all kinds. Some of the better-off actors, like Globe sharer Augustine Philips, had their own (smaller) collections too.

## Written Music

*Elizabethan music was usually scored in several parts, ranging through treble, alto, tenor and bass versions of the same instrument, like a choir today. But it is also possible that sometimes the musicians improvised for the play without any scored music, just as they do at the Globe today. This may help to explain why we have few contemporary scores surviving from the theatres in this period.*

A lute and a sackbut

## Instruments

*Instruments could be played together in different kinds of groups. When instruments of the same family played together it was known as a 'consort'. Strings and wind instruments could also be combined – this kind of group was called a 'broken consort'. In a broken consort the variety was produced by different instruments' sounds as well as by their range of registers.*

Brass instruments such as trumpets and sackbuts (resembling trombones), and woodwind – shawms (like oboes), cornetts and others – would be clearly audible in the outdoor playhouses. Experiments with acoustics in today's Globe suggest that when they played in the open-air playhouses Shakespeare's company probably did not use a broken consort. Instruments that were sedentary and better suited to indoors, such as keyboards and viols, may have been used on stage, for instance to accompany a song sung in an indoor scene, like Feste's song in Orsino's court in *Twelfth Night*.

Meanwhile the intimate acoustics of the indoor theatre tended to favour gentler instruments – mainly keyboards and strings. When a play was transferred indoors from the Globe to the Blackfriars, the parts played by the Globe's brass instruments were taken by woodwinds such as cornetts.

Today's Globe uses replicas of Elizabethan instruments made using old techniques. We commissioned a number of these replicas for display in the exhibition.

©Keith Rogers

*Although ivory cornetts do exist, most of these instruments are made from wood. A curved piece of wood is sliced in half, lengthways, and a central channel along the two halves is gouged out. The two halves are then glued back together and tightly bound in leather. Finally a mouthpiece is added, like one you would find on a modern trumpet.*

# Music at the Globe Today

*©John Tramper*

*The nature of the plays and the architecture of the space itself to a certain extent dictate how you write music for the Globe. You have to take into account the stories of the plays and the nature of the verse, of course; but here if something doesn't work you can't just alter the balance with microphones as you could at another theatre; so the architecture prescribes the kind of music you write and the instruments you can write it for.*

CLAIRE VAN KAMPEN, DIRECTOR OF THEATRE MUSIC

*Musicians on stage at Shakespeare's Globe*

Most of the music used in *Henry V* in the new Globe's opening season was based on an authentic recreation of Elizabethan playhouse music, and was played on reproduction period instruments. But although we do try in some productions to recreate the theatre music of Shakespeare's day, current practice at the Globe encompasses much more than just that search for authenticity.

A wide range of musical styles has already been explored, with composers taking inspiration from African music in *The Winter's Tale* and *Antony and Cleopatra*, and Turkish music in *The Comedy of Errors*. In 1999 folk-rock musician Tim Arnold drew on the music of John Lennon and Glastonbury rock in his creation of a distinctive sound for *Augustine's Oak*; *The Maid's Tragedy* used a five-piece brass ensemble. In 1998 *A Mad World, My Masters* saw a modern violin and a harmonium playing alongside period instruments; while the 2001 season saw the exclusive use of early instruments for *King Lear*, and a contemporary Miles Davis-type jazz band in *Macbeth*.

But whether through period instruments or folk-rock, the music of the Globe's productions aims above all to complement the storylines and to help the audience's appreciation of the text.

The professional musicians at today's Globe work closely with the acting companies. Music is usually played from the Musicians' Gallery above the stage, but sometimes the musicians play on-stage with the actors.

*A display of instruments in the Exhibition*

# The Music of the Spheres

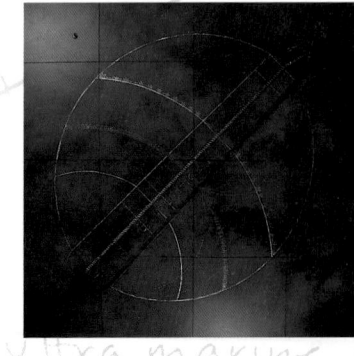

*...his voice was propertied*
*As all the tunèd spheres*
ANTONY AND CLEOPATRA, V.2

*A curtal*

Since the days of Pythagoras – the 6th century BC – music had been associated with the movement of the stars and planets, which were said to be in harmony or discord. Shakespeare makes frequent references to this in his plays;

*If he, compact of jars, grow musical,*
*We shall have shortly discord in the spheres*
AS YOU LIKE IT, II.7

References to 'music of the spheres' were even more meaningful in the context of the Elizabethan playhouses where musicians frequently stood directly below the brightly painted 'heavens' above the stage. This positioning (between earth and the heavens) emphasised the importance of the hierarchical function of music. This may have been a supernatural function, when music heralds an intervention between the Gods and man (a ghost, for instance); or it might have been an inspirational one, such as when music is called on to wake the sleeping or the dead.

*Musicians playing under 'the heavens'*

# Symbols

*Stringed instruments (or 'bas' instruments), which produced sweeter sounds, were thought to suggest heavenly harmonies and balanced reason. Viols, lutes, virginals and harps were played by the nobility and would have been common at court. Louder ('haut') instruments such as cornetts, shawms, trumpets and sackbuts were used for their brighter sounds, and excited a more passionate reaction from the audience.*

*Musical symbolism in one of the Underglobe's ceiling panels*

# Symbolism in the Underglobe

> The Underglobe space is decorated with symbols relating to alchemy, astrology, astronomy, the kabbalah and other ancient and mystical symbolic systems with which Shakespeare and the decorators of theatres were familiar.

Artist Erin Sorensen worked closely with the Globe's Artistic Director Mark Rylance to produce designs for the walls, the columns and eight magnificent ceiling panels which would reflect the importance of such symbolic language to Shakespeare's work and the Globe itself.

*The Underglobe decoration is an abstracted, contemporary, purified representation of the symbolism of historic stage decoration. This includes areas dedicated to the physical and metaphysical planes, and to the transition between the two. This representation uses colour, finishes and space in a symbolic way.*

*In the columns that link the green earth to the heavenly ceiling, one can witness the alchemical process of purification; this is displayed in the upward movement and transition of lower base metals to the higher, purer gold. This transition leads the viewer up to the heavenly colours of the ceiling panels, which represent divine and elemental intelligence and order through sacred geometry and alchemical symbolism. A variety of metal finishes are displayed to reinforce the alchemic process and to entice the play of light.*

ERIN SORENSEN, UNDERGLOBE ARTIST

*Symbolic figures in two of the Underglobe's ceiling panels*

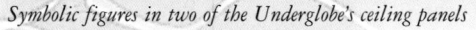

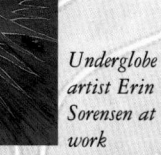

*Underglobe artist Erin Sorensen at work*

This ceiling panel, for instance, shows the kabbalistic tree, whose symbolic language was incorporated into the decoration of the theatre stage. It shows the celestial realm ('the heavens') at the top, and earth/hell below, and is flanked by two columns which in the theatre represent Mars and Venus. This same pattern may also have been used by Shakespeare in his writing, with – for example – the different characters in *Much Ado About Nothing* representing six elements of this symbolic relationship.

# The Oak

*When our houses were builded of willow, then had we oaken men; but now that our houses are come to be made of oak, our men are not only become willow, but a great many ... altogether of straw...*

WILLIAM HARRISON, 1577

*English oak has always stood for strength and long life. The sculptured oak tree that surprises the visitor at the foot of the stairs, represents the enduring nature of Shakespeare's work. It also symbolises the foundation upon which the present Globe stands, since it is directly under the great oak pillars of the stage and, like them, seems to rise from the rooted earth to support the painted ceiling representing the heavens.*

The Theatre above is a place for listening, so it is fitting that standing under the oak you can hear the varied voices and music of the Exhibition all around.

©Nik Milner

The oak

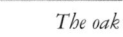

Two dormice in the Underglobe oak

*Heart of oak are our ships,*
*Heart of oak are our men...*
DAVID GARRICK

Buried in a glass-topped, circular vault on the stairs is a collection of time-capsules; these were filled by children from over three hundred Globelink schools, who raised money to build the 'heavens' canopy above the Globe stage. These capsules will be dug up and opened in 2047.

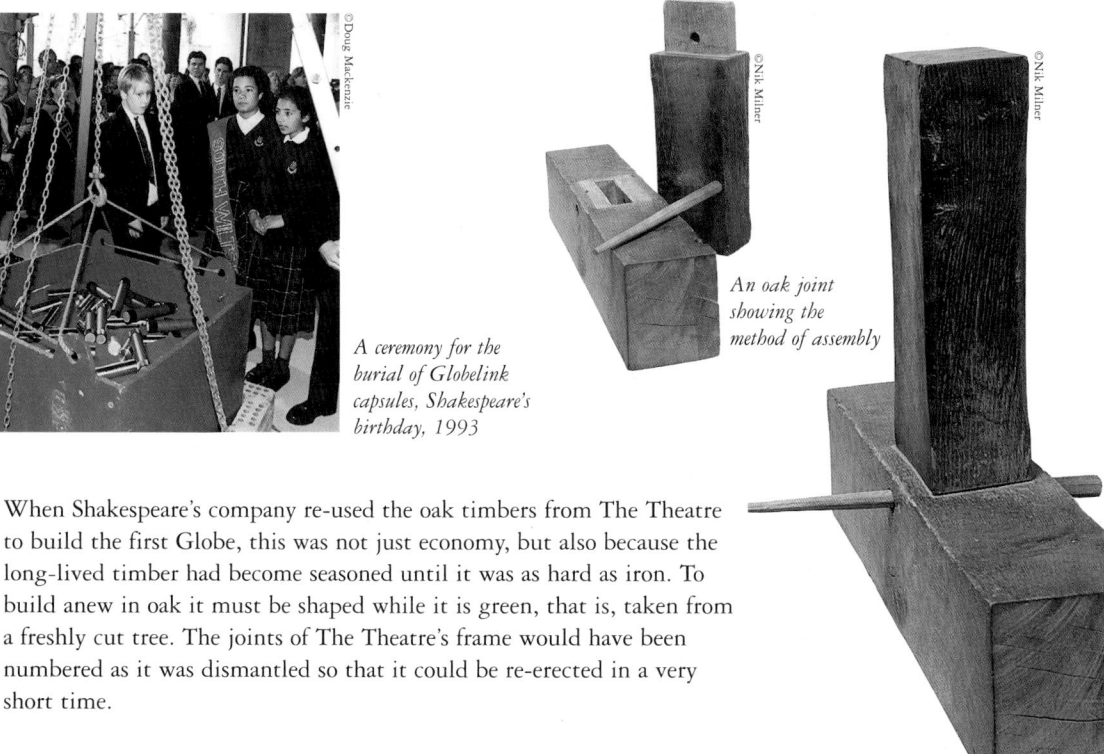

*A ceremony for the burial of Globelink capsules, Shakespeare's birthday, 1993*

*An oak joint showing the method of assembly*

When Shakespeare's company re-used the oak timbers from The Theatre to build the first Globe, this was not just economy, but also because the long-lived timber had become seasoned until it was as hard as iron. To build anew in oak it must be shaped while it is green, that is, taken from a freshly cut tree. The joints of The Theatre's frame would have been numbered as it was dismantled so that it could be re-erected in a very short time.

Great supporting timbers were usually 'boxed heart'; that is, they were made of oak which was hewn to a square, with the sap-wood (which would decay first) at the corners and the heart of oak at the centre.

39

# Rebuilding the Globe

*When we mean to build,*
*We first survey the plot, then draw the model…*
HENRY IV PART 2, I.3

*Partial excavation of the first Globe site confirmed*
*that it had twenty sides and a diameter of 99 feet*

Our Globe is built following as nearly as possible the methods and measurements of the first Globe. This gives us a vehicle for exploring the original practices of Shakespeare in performance, and allows us to test the space, the acoustics and audience reactions.

## Our Best Guess – Some of the evidence, and our deductions…

Oak framing and lath and plaster walls are traditional methods of building used in houses and barns throughout the country.

From brick foundations rise the oak frames that form the inner and outer ring of the structure, the stair towers, stage and tiring house.

Courtesy of Middle Temple

TIRING HOUSE     FRONS SCENAE     STAGE

*Great halls and other Tudor performance spaces provide evidence of decoration.*
*This picture shows the decorative screens at the entrance to Middle Temple Hall*

40

Philip Henslowe, who ran the Rose theatre, kept records that have been preserved. With his son-in-law Edward Alleyn, he built a rectangular theatre – The Fortune, in Cripplegate – to the north of the city the year after the Globe was built. Peter Streete, the builder of The Globe, also built the Fortune and his contract refers more than once to The Globe. It was therefore an important piece of documentary evidence for the reconstruction of the theatre.

*Arendt van Buchell's copy of Johannes de Witt's sketch of The Swan, 1596, believed to be the only surviving representation of the interior of an Elizabethan playhouse.*

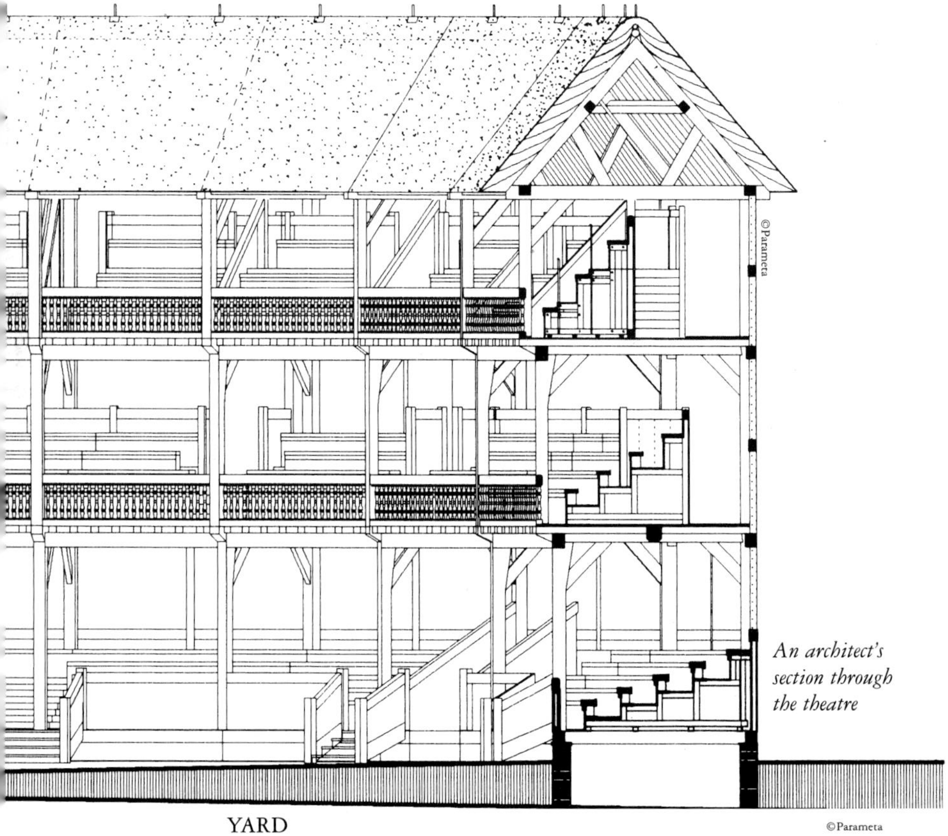

The frame of the saide howse to be sett square and to containe ffowerscore foote of lawfull assize everye waie square withoutt and fiftie five foote of like assize square everye waie within, with a good suer and stronge foundacion of pyles, brick lyme and sand bothe without and within, to be wroughte one foote of assize att the leaste aboue the grounde; And the saide fframe to conteine three stories in heighth, the first or lower storie to conteine Twelve foote of lawfull assize in height, the second Storie Eleaven foote of lawfull assize in height, and the third or vpper Storie to conteine Nyne foote of lawful assize in heighth; All which Stories shall conteine Twelve foote and a halfe of lawfull assize in breadth throughoute, besides a jettey forwardes in either of the saide two vpper Stories of Tenne ynches of lawfull assize, with ffower convenient divisions for gentlemens roomes, and other sufficient and convenient divisions for Twoe pennie roomes, with necessarie seates to be placed and sett, as well in those roomes as througheoute all the reste of the galleries of the saide howse, and with suchelike steares, conveyances & divisions withoute & within, as are made & contryved in and to the late erected Plaiehowse on the Banke in the saide parishe of Ste Saviours called the Globe; With a Stadge and Tyreinge howse to be made, erected & settupp within the said fframe, with a shadowe or cover over the saide Stage; and which Stadge shall conteine in Length Fortie and Three foote of lawfull assize and in breadth to extende to the middle of the yarde of the saide howse; The same Stadge to be paled in belowe with good, stronge and sufficyent new oken bordes; **Ans** also all the saide fframe and the Stairecases thereof to be **sufficyently** enclosed without with lathe, lyme & haire, and the gentlemens roomes and Twoe pennie roomes to be seeled with lathe lyme and haire; **And** the saide howse to be made and doen according to the manner and fashion of the saide howse called the Globe saveinge only that all the princypall and maine postes of the saide fframe and Stadge forwarde shalbe square and wroughte palasterwise, with carved proporcions called Satiers to be placed & sett on the topp of evry of the same postes

*An architect's section through the theatre*

© Parameta

YARD

© Parameta

41

*Jon Greenfield*

*Peter McCurdy*

Studying historical records and existing old timber-frame buildings was one thing, actually building the Globe was quite another undertaking, especially when there was only a little money in the bank. The idea of 'Self-build' was conceived, which meant working a little at a time, creating the Globe frame by frame as oak was donated, and constructing the surrounding buildings whenever concrete could be mixed and bricks laid. Having something to show, something even to dedicate with ceremony or with performance, however minimal the surroundings, certainly helped to raise money, and seemed to be in the spirit of the first Elizabethan companies.

*The Globe roo[f] frame is pre-assembled*

By 1996 the Globe project was well-known to builders and workmen around the country, and it was common for cement trucks to make their way down to Bankside with a donation if ever they found themselves with any materials to spare after a delivery. Much of the concrete for the Underglobe's pillars was obtained in this way.

And thus it was, that under close professional supervision by architect, carpenter and builders, the Globe complex arose little by little on Bankside to become once again, in Ben Jonson's words, *the glorie of the banke.*

Self-build, however, is not a concept that belongs only to the past. There is a continuing programme of fund-raising to develop the Globe site further.

## The Frame

*Green oak was used for the frame. It will settle, season and become very hard in time. The frame was constructed on the ground, in a disused aircraft hangar at Greenham Common, before being taken apart and re-erected on site. One might expect a wooden-framed building to be less sturdy than those built today using modern techniques and materials, but in fact some timber-framed buildings have lasted more than eight hundred years!*

## The Walls

*The walls are plastered on a base of thin oak laths. The plaster is made from lime, sand and goats' hair and is applied in a series of coats. The whole is then finished with a white lime wash.*

*Plastering the walls*

# The Balusters

*During excavations at the Rose site part of a baluster was found. The balusters on the Globe galleries were made to the same pattern using a traditional pole (or "bodger's") lathe.*

Such a device, set up in woodland, uses a long sapling as a spring with one end of a leather strap attached to it, wound around the piece of wood to be turned, and with the other end fixed to a treadle.

# The Thatch

*Shakespeare's Globe is the first major London building to have a thatched roof since the Great Fire of London in 1666. The builders of the new Globe were able to comply with modern fire regulations by including a sprinkler system and fireproof membrane under the thatch.*

©Cafferty/Lewis

*Turning a baluster on a pole lathe*

*Thatching the gallery roof with reeds*

©Richard Kalina

# The Yard

*Nutshells were found during excavation of the Rose Theatre. They could have come from the residue of soap-making, as we know there was a soap-works at neighbouring Bear Gardens. Soap was made from the oil from hazelnuts or animal fat and ashes (lye). A mix of the waste from soap-making (the hazelnut shells, ash and clinker) plus some silt from the river made the rough surface used on London's roads in the 1590s. This same mixture probably made the soft, waterproof composition that covered the yard. It probably smelt very bad. Today's attempts are more ecologically sound, but experiments in the first few seasons met with only limited success.*

©Reading Photographic Services

43

## The Stage

*The stage, which is very large and high off the ground, is a platform for experiment. Below it is a space sufficiently high for standing, while a trapdoor in the centre allows entrances 'from below'. Traditionally this area was called 'hell'. There is another trapdoor in the ceiling for lowering people or objects down to the stage. The whole area above the stage therefore is 'the heavens'.*

*The stage trap becomes Ophelia's grave in* Hamlet

## The Pillars

*Two massive hollowed-out oak pillars run from below stage-level right up through the stage to support the heavens. After experiment found that the pillars were too near the front to allow actors to move around them effectively, the whole design of the rooms and roof-space above the stage had to be changed. It is this spirit of experiment that continues to be part of life at Shakespeare's Globe.*

*A crane lowers one of the giant pillars into the theatre*

*The statue of Hermione in* The Winter's Tale *is revealed in the central opening.*

## The Tiring House

*Behind the stage there are many of the facilities of a modern theatre, but, as in Shakespeare's day, the tiring house is the place from which actors and musicians enter onto the stage and where performances are stage-managed. It cannot truthfully be called 'backstage' as privileged members of the audience sit in part of the balcony, close to the action and therefore performances are 'in the round'. Actors and musicians can also use the balcony. There are three openings with doors at stage level. They can also be hung with curtains or painted cloths. Large 'properties' such as tables, thrones or beds can be brought on through the large central entrance.*

*The tiring house frame with the carpenters who made it*

# Decoration

*Behold the sumptuous theatre houses, a continual monument to London's prodigality and folly.*

<small>THOMAS WHITE, IN A SERMON, 1577</small>

Many visitors are surprised at the lavish decoration of the stage. The oak pillars are painted to resemble marble and the whole tiring house façade is painted and carved. Changes to the decoration of the whole interior are part of the experiment.

*... supported by wooden columns painted in such excellent imitation of marble that it is able to deceive even the most cunning.*

<small>JOHANNES DE WITT, 1596</small>

*The painted ceiling*

*The stage balcony*

Before the decoration of the present Globe stage with paint and sculpture had begun, some people objected to the idea, believing that it would distract from the acting. It seems however that for many productions the opposite is true; richness of colour, with the absence of other scenery, can delight audiences and satisfy the actors.

45

# The Hangings

*The walls of our houses on the inner sides…be either hanged with tapestry, arras work or painted cloths, wherein either divers histories, or herbs, beasts, knots and such like are stained…*

HARRISON, 1577

©Gwen Cox

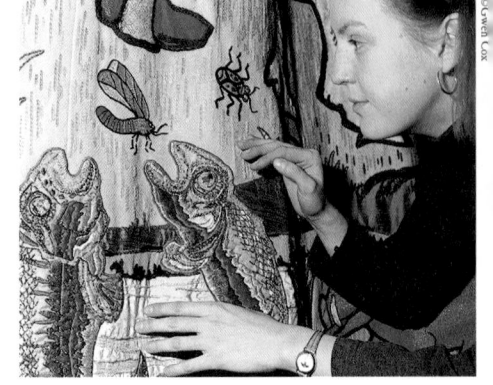

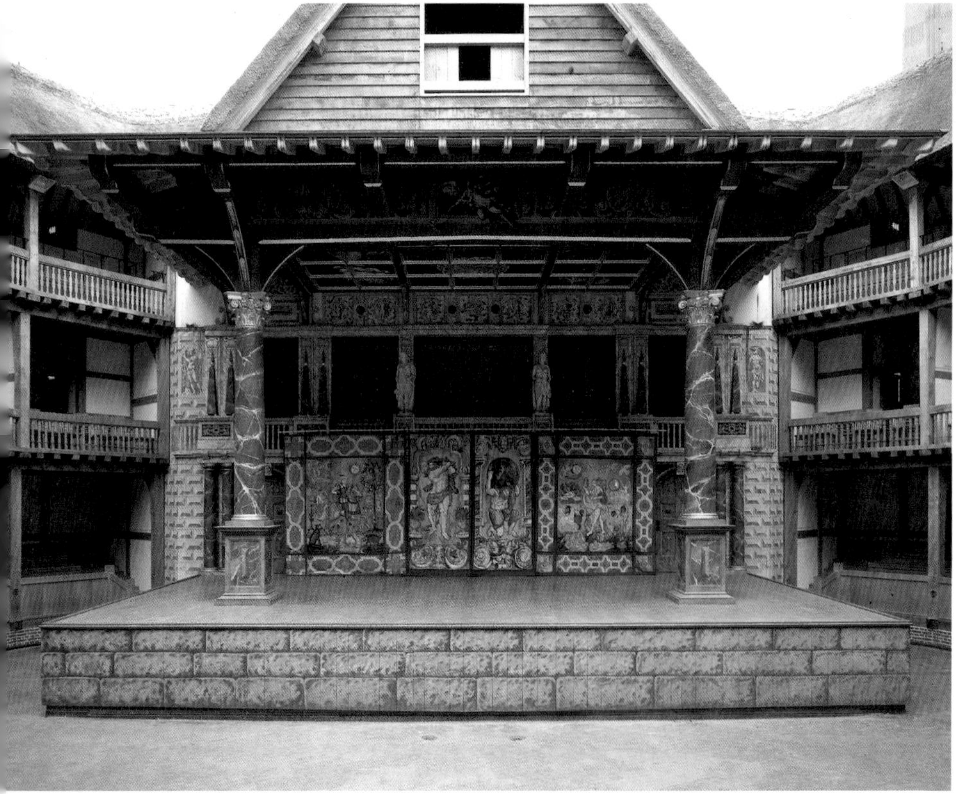

©Richard Kalina

*The New Zealand Hangings in place on the stage, 1997*

Early temporary stages had curtains to provide a background, and indoor playing spaces were often provided with elaborate painted cloths to mask entrances.

In the court masques of Inigo Jones, painted cloths were used to depict a scene.

*First for the scene, was drawn a Landschap, consisting of small woods, and here and there a void place fill'd with huntings…*

BEN JONSON DESCRIBING THE MASQUE OF BLACKNESSE, 1605

Over 500 New Zealand embroiderers worked on the hangings for the Globe. Designed by Dr Raymond Boyce they feature Venus and Adonis, as in Shakespeare's poem, and the figures of Atlas and Hercules who in Greek mythology carried the heavens on their shoulders.

# The story of Atlas and Hercules

*Atlas, the cruel, greedy ruler of Atlantis, was condemned by the Gods to carry the heavens (or the globe) on his shoulders for all eternity.*

For the eleventh of his famous tasks Hercules was to bring back golden apples from a tree that was guarded by Atlas's two daughters. Atlas went to fetch the apples from his daughters, and asked Hercules to hold the globe for him while he was away – but when Atlas returned with the apples he refused to take his burden back. Hercules asked him to hold it, just for a moment, while he adjusted his Nemean lion-skin, and the unsuspecting Atlas agreed.

Free again, Hercules took the golden apples and ran off, leaving the tricked Atlas once more bearing the globe on his shoulders.

The flag that flew above the Globe to announce a performance showed Hercules bearing the round earth upon his shoulders and the motto "totus mundus agit histrionem" ('the whole world moves the actor', or 'all the world's a stage'). The pillars supporting the canopy above the stage are known as the Pillars of Hercules.

*Atlas carrying the globe in one of the panels of the New Zealand Hangings*

©Brett Robertson

©Richard Kalina

*A flag showing Hercules and Atlas carrying the globe on their shoulders flies above the theatre*

In *Hamlet*, Rosencrantz compares the players to 'Hercules'. After all, they do not actually carry the weight of the world on their shoulders, they were not really Kings and Emperors, they just took on the part for a short time, as Hercules did with Atlas's load.

47

# The King's Men

> *Building the first Globe, massive and ornate, was a vast and glorious undertaking.*

When the first Globe was built from the timbers of The Theatre in the early months of 1599, The Theatre's original owners, the Burbages, did not have the money to fund this ambitious construction project; so they appealed to a handful of their co-actors to invest in it themselves. These five shareholders (or 'housekeepers') were John Heminges, Augustine Phillips, William Kemp, Thomas Pope and William Shakespeare.

Like Richard Burbage, these five made up a part of the Lord Chamberlain's Men, a company of players formed when the Lord Chamberlain, Henry Carey, first Baron Hunsdon, granted them his patronage in 1594. There were probably seven actor-sharers in the company, not counting the apprentices and hired men.

*Will Kemp and the signatures of the other Globe shareholders*

*Henry Carey, first Baron Hunsdon, Lord Chamberlain and patron to Shakespeare's company*

The Lord Chamberlain's Men was the most successful company of the day – performing a repertoire that included not only works by Shakespeare but also Jonson, Beaumont and Fletcher and numerous others. Partly because the Lord Chamberlain was responsible for all court performances, the company was regularly invited to perform for Her Majesty in the Christmas season.

Upon the death of the Queen in 1603, her successor, James I, immediately gave his royal name to the company, and by April of that same year he was their official patron. Shakespeare and his fellows had become The King's Men.

Unlike most acting companies today, the King's Men counted among their number actor-musicians and actor-playwrights (like Shakespeare himself). So a production could be put on from first to last within the company – from the actor-playwright writing the play, for performance in a playhouse owned by the actor-sharers, to the adult and boy actors speaking the lines and playing the music.

*Richard Burbage, the leading actor of the King's Men, for whom many of Shakespeare's most famous roles were written*

A company's stock of plays, each one bought from the author in manuscript for perhaps £10, was the most valuable of their possessions. Without any copyright laws they had to guard against their manuscripts getting into other hands. If a company were in dire straits, however, they could sell their plays. During 1594 – after a year of plague – many titles changed hands. When Shakespeare's *Titus Andronicus* was published in that year, it had already been played by four or five different travelling companies. So although acting companies included playwrights among their number, these companies did not only perform those plays produced by their own men. It was not even always clear who did write the plays which were performed…

# The Authorship Debate

*Owing partly to the relatively small number of contemporary documents (certainly a tiny number by modern standards) which link William Shakespeare to the plays generally ascribed to him, for over 150 years many people have believed that another person must have been their true author. In an attempt to enquire into this aspect of the meaning and origin of the Shakespeare plays, our Authorship exhibit introduces what is known about the Stratford actor who is generally accepted as the author, together with the three most researched alternatives.*

The Public Record Office houses most of the important papers relating to William Shakespeare's life, including his will and a number of legal documents. As part of our enquiry into Shakespeare's identity and the authorship question, they have lent us a changing selection of these for display in the Globe Exhibition, in the showcase at the top of the stairs. The Exhibition itself is an enquiry into what is known and conjectured about his life as a working theatre artist in London, and should stimulate visitors' consideration of this long-standing debate.

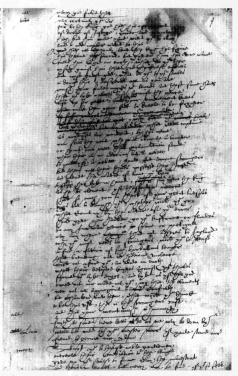

*The manuscript of the play of* Thomas More. *Shakespeare collaborated on this play; this manuscript may be written in his hand.*

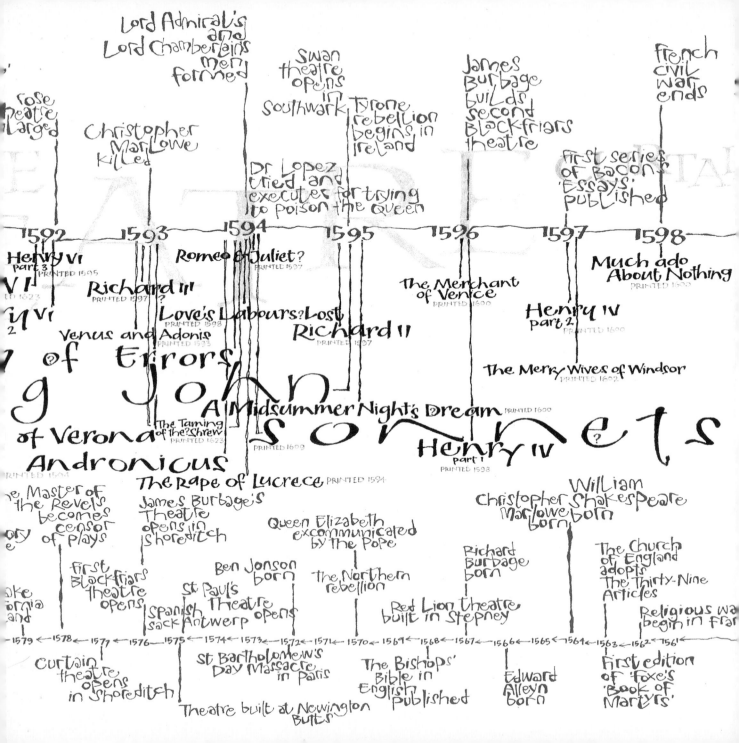

Lord Admiral's and Lord Chamberlain's men formed

Swan theatre opens in Southwark

Tyrone rebellion begins in Ireland

James Burbage builds second Blackfriars theatre

French civil war ends

Rose Theatre enlarged

Christopher Marlowe killed

Dr Lopez tried and executed for trying to poison the Queen

First series of Bacon's 'Essays' published

**1592** **1593** **1594** **1595** **1596** **1597** **1598**

Henry VI part 3 PRINTED 1595

VI PRINTED 1623

in VI 2

Richard III PRINTED 1597?

Romeo & Juliet? PRINTED 1597

Much ado About Nothing PRINTED 1600

Love's Labours? Lost PRINTED 1598

Richard II PRINTED 1597

The Merchant of Venice PRINTED 1600

Henry IV part 2 PRINTED 1600

Venus and Adonis PRINTED 1593

of Errors

The Merry Wives of Windsor PRINTED 1602

g John

of Verona

The Taming of the?Shrew PRINTED 1623

A Midsummer Night's Dream PRINTED 1600

sonnets?

Andronicus PRINTED 1594

Henry IV part 1 PRINTED 1598

The Rape of Lucrece PRINTED 1594

e Master of the Revels becomes censor of plays

James Burbage's Theatre opens in Shoreditch

Queen Elizabeth excommunicated by the Pope

Christopher Marlowe born

William Shakespeare born

First Blackfriars Theatre opens

Ben Jonson born

The Northern rebellion

Richard Burbage born

The Church of England adopts The Thirty-Nine Articles

St Paul's Theatre opens

ke rnia and

Spanish sack Antwerp

Red Lion theatre built in Stepney

Religious wa begin in Fran

←1579← ←1578← ←1577← ←1576← ←1575← ←1574← ←1573← ←1572← ←1571← ←1570← ←1569← ←1568← ←1567← ←1566← ←1565← ←1564← ←1563← ←1562← ←156

Curtain theatre opens in Shoreditch

St Bartholomew's Day Massacre in Paris

The Bishops' Bible in English published

Edward Alleyn born

First edition of 'Foxe's 'Book of Martyrs'

Theatre built at Newington Butts

boy
companies First three
surpliessed books of
'The Faerie Queene
published

cuthbert
Burbage's
lease
of Theatre

1589 — 1590 — 1591

Henry part 1

Henry part

The Comedy

Kin PRINTED 1623

PRINTED 1623

The Two Gentlemen
PRINTED 1623

Titus

Mary Queen
of Scots
executed

Philip Sidney
killed in The
Netherlands

Pope Gre
reforms t
Catholic
calendar

Marlowe's
'Tamburlaine'
acclaimed

Earl of
Leicester
takes army to
The Netherlands

Francis Dr
claims Cali
for Engl

*The timeline spans the years 1552 to 1664. Historical events are in red. Shakespeare's plays are in black. The playhouses are in grey. The position of each play title indicates when it was first published. The play titles appear over the names of the playhouse for which it is believed they were written. Plays written over more than one year span those years. A question mark indicates when a date is uncertain.*

1588 ← 1587 ← 1586 ← 1585 ← 1584 ← 1583 ← 1582 ← 1581 ← 1580 ←

Spanish
Armada
defeated

the Queen's
Men formed

Rose theatre
opens in
Southwark

Drake
completes
his voyage
round the
world

© Kirsten Burke 2001. Chronology devised by Professor Andrew Gurr, Globe Research

*The majority of scholars still agree that it was this actor from Stratford, Mr William Shakespeare/Shakspar, who wrote the plays and poems attributed to him. So why do people doubt that he was the true author? The case often made is as follows:*

*The bust of Shakespeare from Holy Trinity Church, Stratford*

*Mr. William Shakespeare*

*Dates:* 1564-1616
*Background:* Born in Stratford, son of a glover, probably educated at Stratford Grammar School. Married Anne Hathaway in 1583, one daughter in 1583, twins in 1585; a member of the Lord Chamberlain's Men in 1594. A shareholder in the Globe Theatre. Retired to Stratford sometime between 1610 and 1613.

• Though one can be born with the genius to write, one cannot be born with book-learning and experience. What an author experiences in life and learns from study inevitably motivates and demonstrates itself in his work. The little we know of William Shakespeare's life and learning does not marry easily with the content of the plays and poems.

• The Stratford-born actor called William Shakespeare had limited education and no first-hand experience of court life. Where then did he learn so much about philosophy, medicine, law, geography, chivalry, falconry and the host of other subjects used in such detail in the plays?

• The sources for the Shakespeare plays include Italian, Greek, Latin and French texts, many of which had not been translated into English – how did the Stratford man come to be so proficient in so many languages?

• The Stratford man left us no manuscripts, nothing written in his hand but half a dozen signatures. His will does not mention a single book. Does this sound like a man responsible for the greatest writing in the English language?

• When playwright Francis Beaumont died (in the same year as Shakespeare) he was given a grand burial in Westminster Abbey. Shakespeare's friend Ben Jonson likewise. But when Shakespeare died in Stratford, no-one in London even commented on the fact – no tributes were paid, no celebratory verses penned. Was this really the man who had written some of the most popular plays of his day?

### *Edward de Vere, 17th Earl of Oxford*

*Dates:* 1550-1604

*Background:* Aristocratic, educated at Cambridge; a prominent courtier, he toured the continent in 1575, spending nearly a year in Italy.

*Famous for:* His marriage to Lord Burleigh's daughter, numerous celebrated quarrels (with Sir Philip Sidney and others), as a patron to poets, playwrights and acting companies, and for fifteen or so surviving poems of his own.

*The case:* De Vere was a great lover of falconry, music and Italian culture, all of which feature highly in the Shakespeare plays and poems. There are clues in the plays themselves linking them to his life, most prominently a dislike of Lord Burleigh, who may be satirised as Polonius in *Hamlet*; and there are others that may be references to his name. He had easy access to Lord Burleigh's library and his own. For de Vere it would have been politically dangerous – and social suicide – to be known as a playwright.

*Edward de Vere*

### *Francis Bacon, Viscount St. Alban*

*Dates:* 1561-1626

*Background:* Aristocratic, educated at Cambridge; before his time as a law student and Bencher at Gray's Inn, he had spent three years (1576-9) in France.

*Famous for:* Four decades of extraordinary public service as MP, privy counsellor, Attorney-General, Lord Chancellor. A prolific prose writer on history, ethics, politics, mythology and science. Celebrated by Ben Jonson for his great wit and conversation.

*The case:* There is an uncanny similarity between the attitudes, interests and wit of Shakespeare and Bacon. He had a vocabulary consistent only with Shakespeare, and relished the theatre and poetry as a branch of learning, a source of delight, and a means of educating people to virtue. He described himself in a letter as a "concealed poet", and is known to have employed other writers on his behalf. He is the only one of the four leading contenders still alive in 1623 when the First Folio was published.

*Francis Bacon*

### *Christopher Marlowe*

*Dates:* 1564-1593(?)

*Background:* Born in Canterbury, scholarships to King's School Canterbury and Cambridge.

*Famous for:* The seven plays and various poems that bear his name; through these plays he gave birth to Elizabethan blank verse drama. Also for his suspicious death in a tavern brawl in Deptford.

*The case:* Marlowe was a spy on the last day of his bail after being arrested on serious charges of atheism, when he was murdered by a servant of his patron Walsingham in a tavern next to the Thames. His murderer was pardoned and immediately welcomed back into Walsingham's service; Queen Elizabeth herself took charge of all further enquiries into the murder. Hence the suspicion that Marlowe faked his own death, exiled himself to Italy, and continued to write (under the name of his friend and one-time collaborator) with all the intimate knowledge of Italy that the Shakespeare plays demonstrate.

*Portrait of a young man, believed to be Christopher Marlowe*

# Printing

*We have no surviving manuscripts of Shakespeare's work in his own hand (with the possible exception of the* Thomas More *manuscript). It is recorded that Shakespeare's manuscripts were written fluently, with no lines crossed out; on which Ben Jonson commented uncharitably "would he had blotted a thousand..."*

By permission of the Governors of Dulwich College

*The part of Orlando from Robert Greene's* Orlando Furioso

By Permission of the Trustees of Dulwich Picture Gallery

*Edward Alleyn*

A writer's scrawled manuscript would be copied out several times by professional scribes. The original manuscripts, the so-called 'foul papers' remained the property of the theatre company. Playscripts, with costumes, were a company's most valuable asset, in part because each playscript had the crucial signature of the censor, the Master of the Revels, authorising it for performance.

The actors in Shakespeare's company would not have received printed copies of the whole playscript to study; in fact, they may not have seen a complete script at all. Instead, each actor would receive his own lines, with his cues, probably written on a scroll; this was called his *part*. Not allowing actors full scripts helped to avoid plagiarism; the use of parts was also a significant money-saving device, as the copying out of texts by hand could be quite costly. In *A Midsummer Night's Dream*, Francis Flute, who is not used to acting, cannot tell his lines from his cues in the part he has been given:

Flute *"Most radiant Pyramus, most lily-white of hue,*
   *Of colour like the red rose on triumphant briar,*
   *Most brisky juvenal, and eke most lovely Jew,*
   *As true as truest horse that yet would never tire.*
   *I'll meet thee, Pyramus, at Ninny's tomb -"*

Quince *"Ninus' tomb", man! Why, you must not speak that yet; that you*
   *answer to Pyramus. You speak all your part at once, cues and all...*

A MIDSUMMER NIGHT'S DREAM, III.1

There is only one surviving part from the period; this comes from Robert Greene's play *Orlando Furioso,* in which the role of Orlando was probably taken by the great actor Edward Alleyn.

52

We estimate that the Elizabethan-Jacobean period produced at least 2,000 new plays. Of these, fewer than 600 survive in print or manuscript today.

The few that were printed usually did not appear until many years after writing and performance, often not until some time after the playwright's death.

Printers would have used a press much like this one commissioned for the Exhibition.

# Printing

Movable metal type had been in use in Europe since the fifteenth century, when it was developed in Germany by Johann Gutenberg, the man who produced the first printed Bible. It was William Caxton who did the first printing work in England, following the techniques of his Dutch and Belgian contemporaries, as well as those of Gutenberg himself.

In many ways the printing techniques being used in Elizabethan England were not much different from those being used up to the twentieth century.

*The typefounder*

MANUSCRIPTS
PRINTERS WERE USUALLY GIVEN MANUSCRIPT COPIES OF THE COMPLETE PLAY, FROM THOSE HELD BY THE COMPANY. SOMETIMES THEY WOULD RECEIVE THE AUTHOR'S ORIGINAL 'FOUL PAPERS'. THE 'ALLOWED BOOK', THE COPY OF THE PLAY PASSED BY THE CENSORS, WAS FAR TOO VALUABLE TO BE GIVEN TO THE PRINTERS.

*The papermaker*

## Typesetting

*Thousands of pieces of metal type, each representing an individual letter or common combination, were set by hand in a composing stick, line by line. They were then transferred onto long trays known as 'galleys', to create a page of text ready for printing called a 'forme'.*

Of course, the letters had to be made and set 'the wrong way round', so that when the page came off the press the writing was reversed.

Each word was separated by a metal space, not quite type-high, called a 'chase'. Type could also be combined with woodcuts to illustrate the text.

*Yea, from the table of my memory*
*I'll wipe away all trivial fond records,*
*All saws of books, all forms, all pressures past,*
*That youth and observation copied there.*
HAMLET, I.5

*The book printer*

*The bookbinder*

*This process was much the same all over Europe. These pictures were taken from a 'Book of Trades', produced by the German engraver Jost Amman in 1568.*

# Printing

> *Inking balls applied the ink to the raised pages of type. Dampened paper made from rags (unlike most modern paper) was pressed onto the inked surface by a metal plate pulled down by a large screw onto the forme. The forme would then be slid out from under the press on rails, leaving a freshly printed page.*

This was a slow process, producing only about 250 impressions per hour.

### INK
THE INK WOULD HAVE BEEN A COMBINATION OF LAMPBLACK (THE SOOTY RESIDUE THAT SETTLED INSIDE SMOKY LAMPS) FOR THE PIGMENT, AND VARNISH OR BOILED LINSEED OIL TO FIX IT TO THE PAGE.

# Binding, and Beyond…

> *The folded pages were gathered together and stitched. The spines were strengthened with bands of vellum or cord and glued to pasteboard. The edges could be cut later.*

A book then had to be recorded in the Stationers' Register before it could be officially 'published'. Most were sold in St Paul's Churchyard, where the city's booksellers were based.

### PAPER – QUARTO OR FOLIO?
TO PRODUCE A 'QUARTO' EDITION A LARGE SHEET OF PAPER WOULD HAVE EIGHT BOOK-PAGES PRINTED ONTO IT, FOUR ON EACH SIDE, AND WOULD THEN BE FOLDED INTO QUARTERS BEFORE BINDING. FOR A FOLIO EDITION, PAPER OF THE SAME SIZE WOULD HAVE JUST FOUR BOOK-PAGES PRINTED ON IT AND WOULD BE FOLDED JUST ONCE; SO A FINISHED FOLIO EDITION WOULD, OF COURSE, BE TWICE THE SIZE OF A QUARTO.

Printers did not always have a complete and reliable playwright's text to work from. Many editions were instead made from the company's own versions, which had seen substantial cutting and editing for acting purposes. These editions were usually quite different from (and far shorter than) the playwright had intended.

Of the eighteen editions of Shakespeare's plays published in quarto form during his lifetime, several are thought to have been based on these staged versions. Among these are the first quarto of *Henry V*, published in 1600, and the first quarto of *Hamlet* (formerly called the 'bad' quarto) of 1603 which included the immortal line

## *To be or not to be; ay, there's the point.*

At least Shakespeare's non-dramatic verse fared a little better. In 1593 and 1594 he published two long poems under his own name. Fifteen years later saw the publication of his *Sonnets*. There may have been an earlier edition of these (also published in the 1590s) now lost, but it is the 1609 edition that is used as the basis for all modern editions.

The first collected edition of Shakespeare's dramatic works appeared in 1623, seven years after his death. Printed in folio format this has become known as the First Folio. Some 750 copies of the First Folio were printed – about 250 have survived.

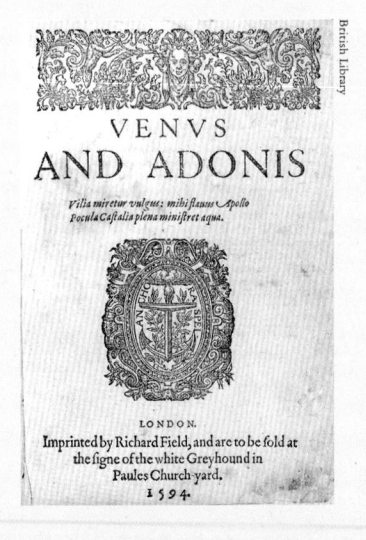

The two men who collected the plays in this edition were John Heminges and Henry Condell. They had both been friends of Shakespeare's, and actors with him in the King's Men, where Heminges may well have been the first actor to play the part of Polonius in *Hamlet*. By 1623 Ben Jonson's *Works* had already been in print in a single volume for seven years, so – they must have thought – why not Shakespeare's too?

They collected thirty-six of his plays, which they divided into sections of Comedies, Histories and Tragedies. This collection included almost all the plays now ascribed to Shakespeare; apart from some collaborative work, only *Pericles* was missing, and this was added in a later edition.

Jonson was among those asked to write 'Commendatory Verses'. The poem he produced for the edition included the famous line

*The 'Droeshout' portrait of Shakespeare, from the title page of the First Folio.*

# *He was not of an age, but for all time.*

*Contents*　　*List of players*

Other prefatory material included an engraved portrait of Shakespeare (the so-called 'Droeshout' portrait) and a list of the "Principall Actors in all these Playes". William Jaggard, a printer based at the Barbican in London, was selected to produce the volume. This edition appeared towards the end of 1623, unbound, probably priced at 15s.

Outside the Guildhall Library in the City of London today, there is a monument to John Heminges and Henry Condell. The inscription reads "To their disinterested affection, The world owes all that it calls Shakespeare". Without these two men, half of Shakespeare's plays might never have appeared in print. It is no coincidence that most of those works of Shakespeare's not included in the First Folio are now 'lost' plays.

# The Editor's Choice

*We often take the accuracy and authenticity of the printed word for granted. But to do this with Shakespeare's work is unwise; we cannot assume that an edition we read or study or use for performance is just as Shakespeare wrote it. Each line of Shakespeare presents an editor with a dozen choices, and his decisions can significantly affect the final result.*

*In the exhibition visitors can edit their own versions of a scene from* Hamlet. *They can ask the same questions and make the same choices as any modern editor.*

*These are just a few of the choices which have to be made by any editor of Shakespeare today:*

1) Which one of the three early editions should serve as a basis for our edition? If the choice is neither of the quartos but the 1623 folio, it looks like this:

*Enter Hamlet.*
*Ham.* To be, or not to be, that is the Queſtion:
Whether 'tis Nobler in the minde to ſuffer
The Slings and Arrowes of outragious Fortune,
Or to take Armes againſt a Sea of troubles,
And by oppoſing end them : to dye, to ſleepe
No more ; and by a ſleepe, to ſay we end
The Heart-ake, and the thouſand Naturall ſhockes
That Fleſh is heyre too? 'Tis a conſummation
Deuoutly to be wiſh'd. To dye to ſleepe,
To ſleepe, perchance to Dreame ; I, there's the rub,

---

2) Having chosen our source, should the font and spelling be modernised to make it easier to read? It may then look like this:

**HAMLET**
To be, or not to be, that is the Question;
Whether 'tis Nobler in the mind to suffer
The Slings and Arrows of outrageous Fortune,
Or to take Arms against a Sea of troubles,
And by opposing end them: to die, to sleep
No more ...

---

3) Shakespeare rarely used stage directions and never made act or scene divisions, but if this is an edition for actors or scholars, they could be useful. Choosing what to put as a stage direction can suggest very different ideas.

For example, compare the simple

*Exeunt. Enter Hamlet.*

with the more evocative

*Claudius and Polonius hide behind the arras.*
*Enter Hamlet, deep in contemplation.*

---

4) Finally, changing the punctuation can completely alter the sense and rhythm of a phrase; compare this

with the original punctuation

*To die, to sleep -*
*No more - and by a sleep to say we end*
*The heartache, and the thousand natural shocks*
*That flesh is heir to. 'Tis a consummation*
*Devoutly to be wished. To die, to sleep -*
*To sleep - perchance to dream. Aye, there's the rub.*

*to die, to sleep*
*No more; and by a sleep, to say we end*
*The heart-ache, and the thousand Natural shocks*
*That Flesh is heir to? 'Tis a consummation*
*Devoutly to be wished. To die to sleep,*
*To sleep, perchance to Dream, aye, there's the rub, ...*

# QUOTING SHAKESPEARE

IF YOU CANNOT UNDERSTAND MY ARGUMENT, AND DECLARE: *it's Greek to me,* you are quoting Shakespeare. IF you claim to be *more sinned against than sinning,* you are quoting Shakespeare. IF you act *more in sorrow than in anger,* if your *wish is father to the thought,* if your lost property has *vanished into thin air,* you are quoting Shakespeare. IF you have ever refused *to budge an inch* or suffered from *green-eyed jealousy,* if you have *played fast and loose,* if you have been *tongue-tied – a tower of strength – hoodwinked* or *in a pickle,* if you have *knitted your brows – made a virtue of necessity,* insisted on *fair play – slept not one wink – stood on ceremony – danced attendance* on your *lord and master – laughed yourself into stitches,* had *short shrift – cold comfort,* or *too much of a good thing,* if you have *seen better days,* or lived *in a fool's paradise,* why, be that as it may, *the more fool you,* for it is a *foregone conclusion* that you are *as good luck would have it,* quoting Shakespeare. IF you think it is *early days* and clear out *bag and baggage,* if you think *it is high time,* and that *that is the long and short of it,* if you believe that *the game is up,* and that *truth will out,* even if it involves your *own flesh and blood,* if you *lie low* till *the crack of doom* because you suspect *foul play,* if you have *teeth set on edge at one fell swoop – without rhyme or reason,* then *to give the devil his due* if the *truth were known* for surely you have a *tongue in your head,* you are quoting Shakespeare. EVEN IF you bid me *good riddance* and *send me packing,* if you wish I was *dead as a doornail,* if you think I am an *eyesore* – a *laughing stock* – the *devil incarnate* – a *stony-hearted villain* – *bloody-minded,* or a *blinking idiot,* then *by Jove – O Lord – tut, tut! – For goodness' sake – what the dickens! – but me no buts – it is all one to me,* for you are quoting Shakespeare...

BERNARD LEVIN

REPRODUCED BY KIND PERMISSION OF THE TIMES NEWSPAPER © SET IN TIMES CLASSIC, THE LIVERY OF THE TIMES.

# Speaking Shakespeare

*We do not know much about how English was spoken aloud in Shakespeare's day. What little we do know we can deduce from spelling and rhyme, and from certain other sources such as* The English Primrose, *a book about how to relate spelling to pronunciation, produced by Southwark schoolmaster Richard Hodges in 1644.*

*The English Primrose, a book explaining how to relate spelling to pronunciation*

As with much of the Globe's 'reconstructive' work, we have to use our limited evidence to assemble a 'best guess' theory.

This is a phonetic transcription of how – according to one such theory – a passage of Shakespeare might have sounded when it was spoken from the Globe stage for the first time over four centuries ago.

| | |
|---|---|
| *Frinds, Roomuns, coontrimun, lend me yurr errs.* | Friends, Romans, countrymen, lend me your ears. |
| *Oy coom too berry Sayzurr, nut too preyse im.* | I come to bury Caesar, not to praise him. |
| *Thee eevul that men doo livz aafturr theym,* | The evil that men do lives after them, |
| *The gewd iz awft inturrid with thyr boonz.* | The good is oft interrèd with their bones. |
| *Soo let ut bee with Sayzurr. The nerbl Brootus* | So let it be with Caesar. The noble Brutus |
| *Eth toowld yu Sayzurr wuz ambishius.* | Hath told you Caesar was ambitious. |
| *If it ware soo, it wuz a greevus fawlt,* | If it were so, it was a grievous fault, |
| *Und greevusly hath Sayzurr arnserrd it.* | And grievously hath Caesar answered it. |
| *Heerr, undr leeve uv Brootus un the rest –* | Here, under leave of Brutus and the rest - |
| *Fur Brootus iz un onawrubl mun –* | For Brutus is an honourable man, |
| *Soo aar thay ol, ol onawrubl men –* | So are they all, all honourable men - |
| *Cum Oy too speek in Sayzurrs fyoonurrul.* | Come I to speak at Caesar's funeral. |
| *Hee wuz mahy frind, faythful un djust too mee,* | He was my friend, faithful and just to me, |
| *But Brootuz sez hee wuz ambishius,* | But Brutus says he was ambitious, |
| *Un Brootus iz un onawrubl mun.* | And Brutus is an honourable man. |

The history of Shakespeare in performance is a continuing process of reinterpretation that spans the centuries from his own time to ours. Nothing illustrates this more clearly than to hear the actual voices of actors speaking across the years since recording techniques began in the 1890s.

After all, Shakespearean language is best appreciated when spoken aloud. So there are booths in the Underglobe where visitors can hear many famous actors speaking lines from Shakespeare's plays; these recordings come from the collection in the National Sound Archive at the British Library.

In the Exhibition you can read and speak lines in scenes cued by recorded actors – a sort of 'karaoke' Shakespeare! – and hear the performance played back to you.

*Speak the speech, I pray you, as I pronounced it to you, trippingly on the tongue; but if you mouth it, as many of your players do, I had as lief the town-crier spoke my lines. Nor do not saw the air too much with your hand, thus; but use all gently: for in the very torrent, tempest, and – as I may say – whirlwind of passion, you must acquire and beget a temperance, that may give it smoothness.*

*HAMLET, III.2*

*The goal of an actor is to sound impassioned but natural. As Master of Verse I invite them to see how 'speech-like' the verse is, how the rhythms and breaks in the verse correspond to the rhythms and breaks in extemporised speech; if they observe how one verse line follows another they can achieve both clarity and spontaneity. Unlike prose, which is frequently harder to work, verse has a quality of immediacy, of expressing 'the moment'. Whether dealing with verse or prose, the actors and I work to try to reveal as much of the richness of our texts as we can – our ultimate aim should always be to allow the dramatist's insights to come alive for an audience.*

GILES BLOCK, MASTER OF VERSE

# Dressing the Actors

*In Shakespeare's day actors specialised in certain types of characters. Clowns, women's roles and kings would all have distinctive costumes and the Roman plays in the repertoire would be dressed accordingly.*

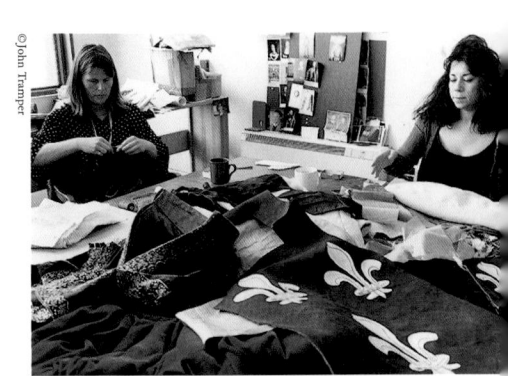

©John Tramper

*Costumes for* Henry V *being made.*

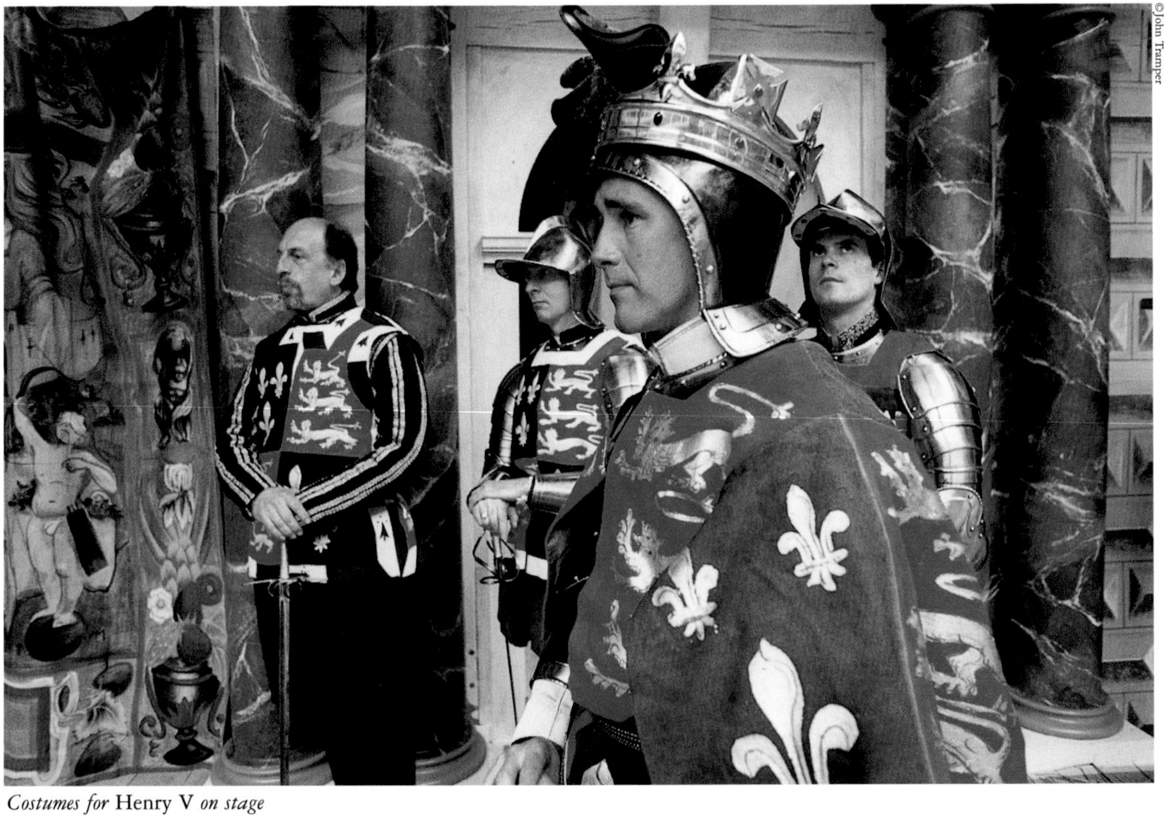

©John Tramper

*Costumes for* Henry V *on stage*

In today's Globe some plays are presented as 'authentic' productions, that is, exploring aspects of original practice; others may have simulated Renaissance (Elizabethan/Jacobean) dress and yet others may be designed in modern dress or use costumes to create their own imaginary 'other worlds'.

In authentic productions every care is taken to research not only the appearance of a costume but also the detail of stiffening and underclothes, fabric, stitching and decoration.

Daylight performances and the proximity of the audience make detail and richness doubly important. The underlying construction of a period costume, such as corsets for the men playing women, can give an actor a different stance and movement.

*Cleopatra's bodice*

*Detail of the embroidery*

*Mark Rylance as Cleopatra*

*The Globe is exciting in terms of clothes because we're always looking for the truth here, but of course there are only ever degrees of authenticity. We want to be as close as we can within the limits of our capabilities and of time and money. Authenticity should never get in the way between the audience and the play, so there are perhaps things we would choose not to do because they would seem too bizarre to a modern audience, too distracting.*

JENNY TIRAMANI, ASSOCIATE DESIGNER

# The Theatre
# Workroom

*In this imaginary workshop, a visitor can see examples of some of the techniques which would have been used to clothe Shakespeare and his fellow-actors.*

Natural dyes were extracted from plants, earths, metals and lichens.

The actor Edward Alleyn, away on tour, writes to his wife: *'I pray you let my orange tawny stockings of woollen be dyed a very good black against I come home, to wear in the winter.'*

Pinking and slashing were ways of making inflexible material such as leather more pliable, and provided additional surface decoration and texture.

The starching of linen was a very new invention, and it was this that allowed ruffs to get larger and larger. A Dutchwoman, Mrs Vanderplasse, charged high prices for the secret of starching ruffs.

Brothel-keeper Anne Turner introduced yellow starch, but after she was implicated in the notorious poisoning of Sir Thomas Overbury and executed while wearing such a ruff, the fashion quickly ended.

A 'poking stick' was heated and used to open up the 'setts' of a ruff.

Lace trimmings and embroidery – often in black or metal threads – were among the myriad popular forms of surface decoration used.

By Shakespeare's day, armour was not much used for warfare, but the theatre could still make use of it.

Today's visitors can try on some of the pieces.

*England, the players' stage of gorgeous attire*
THOMAS NASHE, CHRISTS TEARES OVER IERUSALEM, 1593

Audiences used to seeing the rich and famous wearing elaborate clothes would have expected no less from actors.

Edward Alleyn at The Rose made a list of the costumes in the wardrobe. Nearly a hundred separate costumes are listed. They range from specific costumes for named characters, to simple blue calico gowns.

Most are extremely rich and include robes trimmed with fur and even ermine, a kind of fur whose use was limited by law to royalty. The so-called 'sumptuary laws' had been in existence for many years to limit people's spending on 'sumptuous' things such as clothing. According to these laws, certain fabrics, laces and furs were restricted to the nobility or the very rich.

*It is the English usage for eminent lords or knights at their decease to bequeathe and leave almost the best of their clothes to their serving men, which it is unseemly for the latter to wear, so that they offer them for sale for a small sum to the actors.*
THOMAS PLATTER, 1599

Some people were shocked by the liberties taken by common players in wearing these fine clothes.

Among others in Henslowe's list there are 'antic sutes' which could mean Roman or 'antique' costumes, as well as 'antic' or comedy costumes such as 'Will Somer's Cote'. Will Somers (Summers) was Henry VIII's famous jester, and appears in a play by Thomas Nashe called *Summers Last Will and Testament*.

Many theatre costumes were extremely expensive; there are records of Alleyn and his brother spending over £20 (equivalent to half the monthly takings at The Rose in a good month) on a single cloak.

*Gownes*
hary ye viii gowne
the blak velvett gowne wt wight fure
A crimosin Robe strypt wt gould fact wt ermin
on of wrought cloth of gould
on of red silk wt gould buttens
a cardinalls gowne
wemens gowns
i blak velvett embroyde wt gould
i cloth of gould candish his stuf
i blak velvett lact and drawne out wt wight sarsnett
A blak silk wt red flush
A cloth of silver for pan
A yelow silk gowne
a red silk gowne
angels silk
ii blew calico gowns

*Antik sutes*
a cote of crimosin velvett cutt in payns and embryderd in gould
i cloth of gould cote wt grene bases
i cloth of gould cote wt oraing tawny bases
i cloth of silver cott wt blewe silk and tinsell bases
i blew damask cote the more
a red velvett horsmans cote
a yelow tafata pd
cloth of gould horsmans cote
cloth of bodkin hormans cote
orayng tawny horsmans cot of cloth lact
daniels gowne
blew embroyderde bases
will somers cote
wight embroydr bases
gilt lether cot
ii hedtirs sett wt stones

# Properties

In 1598 the list of properties at
The Rose contained a great many
classical objects, from Cupid's
bow and quiver and Cerberus's
three heads, to pieces of scenery
such as mossy banks, tombs and
a hell-mouth.

©Nik Milner

*The costume display in the Exhibition is constantly
changing; the items displayed come from our unique
collections of theatre costumes and original fabrics.*

*j rocke, j cage, j tombe, j Hell mought*
*j tombe of Guido, j tombe of Dido, j bedstead.*
*vjjj lances, j payer of stayers for Fayeton*
*jj stepells, & j chyme of belles & j beacon*
*j hecfor (heifer) for the playe of Faeton, the limes dead.*
*j globe,& j golden scepter, jjj clobes*
*jj marchpanes, & the sittie of Rome.*
*j gowlden flece, jjrackets, j baye tree.*
*j wooden hatchett, j lether hatchete.*
*j wooden canopie, owlde Mahametes head.*
*j lyone skin, j beares skyne & Faetones lymes, & Faeton charete,& Argosse heade*
*j Nepun forcke & garland*
*j cosers stafe, Kentes woden leag.*
*Jerosses head & rainbowe, j little alter*
*vjjj viserdes, Tamberlyne bridell, j wooden mattook*
*Cupedes bowe & quiver, the clothe of the Sone & Mone*
*j bores heade & serberosse jjj heads*
*j Cadeseus, jj mose bankes, & j snake.*
*jj fanes of feathers, Belendon stable, j tree of gowlden appelles, tantelouse tre, jx eyorn targates.*
*j copper targate, & xviii foyles*
*jjj wooden targates, j greve armer.*
*j syne for Mother Redcap, ,j buckler*
*Mercures wings, Tasso picter, j helmet with a dragon, j shelde with jjj lyones j elme bowle*
*j chayne of dragons, j gylte speare.*
*jjj coffines, j bulles head and j vylter*
*jjj tymbrells, j dragon in Fostes (Faustus)*
*j lyone,jj lyones heades j great horse with his leages, j sack-bute.*
*j whell and frame in the Sege of London*
*j paire of rowghte gloves.*
*j poopes miter*
*jjj Imperial crownes, j playne crowne.*
*j gostes crown, j crown with a sone.*
*j frame for the heading in Black Jone*
*j blacke dogge*
*j cauderm for the Jewe*

# Elizabethan Actors in Costume: characters possibly from *Titus Andronicus*

*This drawing by Henry Peacham is said to date from 1595. It is believed to be the only contemporary depiction of a scene (or a composite of scenes) from a Shakespeare play. So it is a vital piece of evidence about the kinds of clothes actors may have worn on stage in Shakespeare's day.*

*To an Elizabethan audience, the style of dress and objects such as crowns or weapons would help to establish the status of a character.*

By permission of the Marquess of Bath, Longleat

*From left to right:*

The guards' costume is very appropriate for quick changes. Basic Elizabethan dress with old-fashioned half armour is enough to tell us that they are armed guards; while the halberds, scimitar, sashes and plumed headgear bring a foreign touch to the costume.

Titus wears a recognisably Roman breastplate and laurel wreath with a sash and carries an unusual spear. The sash may represent a toga, or might simply suggest that Titus is a military man.

Tamora, Queen of the Goths, played by a young man, wears what appears to be a smock or a loose gown with embroidered sleeves, a long veil and a crown. The smock would suggest a character who is mad; the veil and crown, being unlike any English dress, would denote a foreign queen of an earlier time.

The kneeling figures of Tamora's sons wear less authentic Roman breastplates and skirts and one has a sash.

Aaron, the moor, has Roman dress, apart from the sleeves that are long, perhaps to minimise the need for 'blacking up'. As far as we know there were only white actors in the company.

# Shoes

*A Shakespearean theatre wardrobe would have had need for a great many shoes – sandals and buskins, or boots, for 'ancient' characters as well as a wide variety of contemporary shoes.*

Actors may well have used their own clothing on stage, including footwear; certainly footwear, like tailoring, was often individually made for each customer. Nowadays Globe productions use handmade shoes based on original designs.

Working men needed one good pair of stout shoes made to last a lifetime.

Shoes were not always made either left or right. Wearing shaped them to the feet.

©Nik Milner

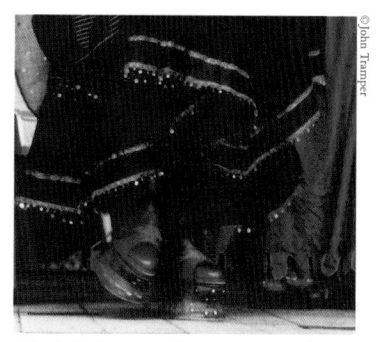

©John Tramper

*Mark Rylance as Cleopatra wears chopines*

Fancy shoes could be worn with 'pattens' or 'chopines' to raise them above the mud.

*…your ladyship is nearer Heaven than when I saw you last, by the altitude of a chopine.*
HAMLET, II.2

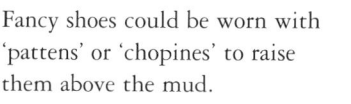

# Headdresses

*Men and women wore very similar hats, flat bonnets made of leather, cloth or knitted fabric, and tall hats with small brims sometimes made of felt.*

Women and old men wore coifs or linen caps indoors and put a hat on top when going outdoors.

Hats were worn indoors and out, except as a mark of deep respect such as being in the presence of royalty or at church. Hats were 'doffed' as a greeting to friend or stranger, but returned to the head at the end of the courtesy.

In this passage from *Hamlet*, the courtier Osric is obviously fawning on the prince:

Osric    *Sweet Lord, if your lordship were at leisure, I should import a thing to you from his majesty.*

Hamlet  *I will receive it, sir, with all diligence of spirit, Put your bonnet to his right use; 'tis for the head*

HAMLET, V.2

Queen Elizabeth wore a wig in old age. Wigs would often have been worn in the theatre, especially by the men and boys playing girls. They were usually made from real hair, but may sometimes have been made from silk.

*Toby Cockerell wears a wig as Portia in* Julius Caesar.

# Modern Design at the Globe

*Shakespeare's Globe is a living, growing organisation. It does not present only authentically costumed plays but also gives full rein to directors and designers to work completely freely within the context of a production.*

Visiting companies and student productions add to the range of new and exciting design ideas. Companies from overseas introduce us to their own traditions.

*A modern-dress* Cymbeline *at the Globe, 2001*

Macbeth *in modern dress, 2001*

# Moving Ahead

*The Theatre and the Exhibition are now finished, but there are many aspects of Shakespeare's Globe still to complete if we are to realize Sam Wanamaker's vision.*

©Nik Milner

The temporary premises for Globe Education on the site fall some way short of the great demands now made upon it by schools and colleges from the U.K. and overseas. Workshop rooms, rehearsal studios and a suite of library and study facilities are all badly needed if we are to meet the educational demands of the 21st century.

Moreover, unlike other major theatres presenting Shakespeare in the U.K., we receive no state subsidy for our artistic and educational operations. This makes it all the more important that we make the most of the commercial potential of our ancillary activities. A public bar and better banqueting facilities for client entertainment, a second shop, an enlarged public access area and the administrative space to support these additional services are all vital if we are to fund our developing educational and artistic programmes.

At the time of writing (summer 2001), we are seeking £9.5 Million to realize these aims. Donations from great corporations and individuals have all contributed to the £1 Million we have raised so far and there are many ways in which we can publicly acknowledge gifts both great and small.

## Playing a part
### The Supporting Wall

*The Supporting Wall is a prominent feature on the way out of the exhibition. Add your signature and you will be immortalized at Shakespeare's Globe. All signatures are enlarged and etched on to copper plaques covering the wall. This wall will be seen by the millions of visitors visiting the Globe in the years ahead and is already a focal point in guided tours of the theatre.*

## Play Patronage

*Support a production at the Globe Theatre and share your enjoyment of our work with thousands of other theatre lovers from across the world. Only 100 Play Patronages are made available for each production and all Patrons enjoy a wonderful array of benefits and special acknowledgment in a Globe production programme.*

## Corporate support

*For the corporate donor, there is a wealth of imaginative naming opportunities. Among these are the planned education premises – each of its workshop spaces, the teachers' resource room and two rehearsal studios – and the library and research centre, likely to become one of the world's leading centres for the academic study of Shakespeare in performance.*

## The Corporate Access Scheme

*Join the Globe Corporate Access Scheme and reap the benefits of membership with significant discounts on corporate hospitality at the Globe. Members receive priority access to the best house seats and private boxes, reductions on function room hire charges and other exclusive offers.*

For further details, contact the appeals office on 020 7902 1400.

### The Friends of Shakespeare's Globe

The Friends of Shakespeare's Globe was set up in 1985 to establish a membership scheme for those wishing to support the Globe. Each year the Friends make donations towards the Globe project and sponsor a special access scheme in the theatre. Joining the Friends will allow you to take advantage of the following:

- Free admission to Shakespeare's Globe Exhibition and reduced rate for a guest
- Priority booking for all theatre performances
- Free copies of the Globe's quarterly magazine *Around the Globe* and the Friends' newsletter 'Cuesheet'
- Concessionary admission to Globe Education's staged readings, workshops and talks
- Access to exclusive events, activities and visits organized by the Friends

Contact the Friends' office for further details:
The Friends of Shakespeare's Globe,
21 New Globe Walk,
London SE1 9DT
Telephone 20 7902 5970
email friends@fosg.org
Join online at www.shakespeares-globe.org/friends
Registered charity, no. 800716

# Globe-to-Globe

*Shakespeare is now accepted as a writer who belongs to the whole world, an artist who uses a language that speaks to all people, but he began as an Englishman, a writer who wrote in English. So it is fitting that it is here on Bankside, Shakespeare's working home, that we have an international centre dedicated to exploring his enduring influence around the world, and his evolving role as a truly global artist.*

*Kathakali King Lear,* 1999

Shakespeare's Globe has affiliations with six **Shakespeare Globe Centres** around the world, in the USA, Canada, Japan, Germany, Australia and New Zealand. Each plays a significant part in the cultural life of its own country, and contributes to the Globe's work in numerous ways, through Friends' programmes, educational activities, fundraising projects, the International Artistic Fellowship, or diverse other projects such as the magnificent New Zealand Hangings (see p.46).

We also have links to several of the reconstructed Elizabethan playhouses around the world, from Tokyo to Gdansk.

**GlobeLink**, Globe Education's international membership scheme, allows students and teachers from all over the world to keep up-to-date with news and activities at the Globe via the internet. Through 'Adopt an Actor' they can follow a Globe actor's progress from first rehearsals right through to performance.

*Romeu e Julieta,* 2000

*Kyogen of Errors,* 2001

*Umabatha: The Zulu Macbeth,* 2001

Each year the Globe hosts a visiting production from abroad. Companies from different cultural traditions are given the opportunity to perform Shakespeare – their way – on the Globe stage. **Globe-to-Globe** productions to date have included a Zulu *Macbeth*, a Cuban *Tempest*, a Kathakali *King Lear*, a Brazilian *Romeo and Juliet* and a Japanese Kyogen *Comedy of Errors*. Each has given us a new and vital perspective on Shakespeare's plays and the potential of his theatre.

The Globe's own acting company has taken some of its productions on tour abroad; recent visits have included *As You Like It* and *King Lear* at the Tokyo Globe and *Hamlet* in the Teatro Olimpico, Vicenza.

The **Globe Exhibition** celebrates these international links with temporary exhibitions on international themes; these have included an exhibition about the Elizabethan playing companies' tours of the continent and a collection of Japanese 'Washi' (handmade paper) sculptures representing Shakespearean and Kabuki characters.

*Otra Tempestad,* 1998

# Credits and contact information

Authors - Daniel Hahn and Rosemary Linnell
Editorial Adviser - Nick Robins
Picture Researcher - Daniel Hahn
Project Director - David Marshall

Produced by Ian Wolverson Associates
Designed by DS Print & ReDesign
Printed by Chapel Press

Shakespeare's Globe Publications
ISBN: 0-9536480-1-X

©Richard Kalina

## ACKNOWLEDGMENTS

We would like to thank Ian Smith and Cognitive Applications Ltd for supplying the images
from their interactive displays (pp. 28, 34 & 36); Keith Rogers, Erin Sorensen and Paul
Wells for supplying pictures of their work on the exhibition displays; Tom Deveson, Faith
Evans, Rex Gibson, Heather Neill and Jeanne Strickland for their comments on the
manuscript; Robert Godley for his work on the Bankside picture on pp. 22-3; Dave Farey for
resetting the Bernard Levin quotation on p. 59; and Alice Reynolds for some of the research
material we have used in producing certain sections of this book. We are particularly grateful
to Jerome Monahan for his work on the Education text which appears on pp. 14-17. We are
grateful to all those photographers who have generously allowed us to use their pictures in
the guide, in particular to Sheila Burnett, Donald Cooper and Nik Milner; and to the actors
and others who have allowed us to quote from their accounts of their experiences of working
here. We would like to thank all the staff of the International Shakespeare Globe Centre,
whose contibutions to the text and illustrative material have been invaluable.

Finally we would like to recognise the work of all those people in Globe Education, the
Theatre Department, the Exhibition and Administration, who make up the Globe family.
The fact that it is possible for you to visit this theatre, to join a workshop or hear a play is
thanks to them. It is their dedication which enables each visitor to find a path to the Globe.

Front cover: John Tramper: *Antony and Cleopatra*, 1999
Back cover: British Library: Moyses Walens, *Album Amicorum*

## Contacting us

Shakespeare's Globe
21 New Globe Walk
London SE1 9DT
www.shakespeares-globe.org
Exhibition: (020) 7902 1500
Main Switchboard: (020) 7902 1400
Theatre Box Office: (020) 7401 9919

Globe Education bookings:
'Lively Action' (020) 7902 1433
Continuing Education (020) 7902 1430

Shakespeare's Globe Cafe: (020) 7902 1576
Shakespeare's Globe Restaurant: (020) 7928 9444